THE PURPLE AND THE SCARLET

The Purple and the Scarlet

by
GUY SCHOFIELD

A.D. 39-155
The Historical Sequel to the
New Testament

George G. Harrap & Co. Ltd
London Toronto Wellington Sydney

First published in Great Britain 1959
by GEORGE G. HARRAP & CO. LTD
182 High Holborn, London, W.C.1

Reprinted : 1959 *(twice)*; 1960

Composed in Georgian type and printed at the St Ann's Press
Park Road, Altrincham. Made in Great Britain

Preface

THE book we know as the New Testament ends abruptly with Paul captive in Rome, in the year A.D. 62. The curtain is rung down upon no climax. We do not know why Luke stopped writing at that point: "the rest is silence." But what *did* happen afterwards? What contemporary events in the world at large had a bearing on these things? What had been going on, that is not recorded in the Acts of the Apostles, during the period when the disciples were alive? What had happened to Peter and John and the rest? What is known and what is supposition about the immediate future of the Christians? What was earthily real as distinct from the affirmations of faith? What persons unmentioned in the New Testament played a part in the struggle between the Empire and the Cross?

This book is an attempt to tell the story of the next hundred years in a manner acceptable to the general reader; that is, as a narrative with a central theme, linked by the interplay of characters through three generations—to the death of the last Apostolic Father. The picture cannot be complete; it cannot be finally authentic. Factual knowledge is in separated bits, like scattered rocks sticking up in a mobile sea of speculation and drift. For the classification of that knowledge and, as it were, for the geological analysis of those rocks every writer is indebted to the work of tireless scholars in many lands. But in assessing its worth, in interpreting its relationship and making deductions, he is entitled to his own judgment. Such judgment as I have brought to bear here is no more specialized than that of one who, since boyhood, has in one capacity or another dealt in news, its gathering and its testing. It is perhaps not unuseful that a mind practised in such a field should look at the raw material of so dramatic and important a sequence.

I have not interrupted the narrative with copious quotations, neither have I indulged in footnotes nor used references. While this lays me open to criticism, I may fairly reply that to produce another tome heavy with argument, annotation, and document-ary fingerpoint would utterly defeat the end I have in view. The sources and acknowledgments are given in an appendix, and those whose preliminary interest may be stimulated by what I have written can pursue the whole subject, if they wish, in pro-founder works. But I have endeavoured to deal fairly with the reader, and where my own verdict or choice of views is opposed by a substantial body of opinion I have made the fact clear.

My interpretation of events is inevitably opinionative; the choice of emphasis entirely my own. Dates, where the record is uncertain, are those I judge to be correct, or approximately so.

It should be pointed out that modern textual criticism tends to disprove the Papian account of the origin of the Gospels which I have adopted. Even if this were the kind of book in which such a subject could be discussed in detail it would be an impertinence on my part to attempt it. I have taken the line that the assertions made by those who lived within a century of the origin of the documents must be allowed to stand for com-mon historic acceptance until evidence—other than conflicting deductive theory—is forthcoming to the contrary.

I wish to express my gratitude for permission to use copyright material. The prefatory quotation from the *Book of James* is from the translation by Dr M. R. James in his *Apocryphal New Testament* (Clarendon Press, Oxford). Extracts from the letters of Clement and Ignatius are in Kirsopp Lake's translation of *The Apostolic Fathers* (Loeb Classical Library; Heinemann). I have used the English version by H. J. Lawlor and J. E. L. Oulton of *Eusebius* (S.P.C.K.). The letter from Hadrian to Plotina is as translated in *The Life and Principate of the Emperor Hadrian*, by Bernard W. Henderson (Methuen), and the papyrus letter of Ben Kosebah is from *The Dead Sea Scrolls*, by J. M. Allegro (Penguin Books). I have also taken a phrase or two of quotation concerning the trial of Eliezer ben Hyrcanus from *Jesus of Nazareth*, by Joseph Klausner (Allen and Unwin).

GUY SCHOFIELD

Contents

Maps

Mary's Lot

From the Book of James, *an infancy Gospel that was in circulation in the second century*

NOW there was a council of the priests, and they said: Let us make a veil for the Temple of the Lord. And the priest said: Call unto me pure virgins of the tribe of David. And the officers departed and sought and found seven virgins. And the priests called to mind the child Mary, that she was of the tribe of David and was undefiled before God; and the officers went and fetched her. And they brought them into the Temple of the Lord and the priest said: Cast me lots which of you shall weave the gold and the undefiled (white) and the fine linen and the silk and the hyacinthine, and the scarlet and the true purple. And the lot of the true purple and the scarlet fell unto Mary, and she took them and went unto her house.

And Mary took the scarlet and began to spin it. And she took the pitcher and went forth to fill it with water; and lo a voice saying: Hail thou that art highly favoured; the Lord is with thee; blessed art thou among women.

And she looked about her, upon the right hand and upon the left, to see whence this voice should be; and being filled with trembling she went to her house and set down the pitcher, and took the purple and sat down upon her seat and drew out the threads.

Like so many early writings, that account of the Annunciation is unconsciously steeped in symbolism. Mary spinning her threads, all unaware that the Imperial purple of Rome was to be stained with the blood of her son and was to be mingled with the scarlet stream of sacrifice for centuries—how poignant in its prophecy was the lot she drew!

The Imperial Succession

I

The Golden Shore

IN the spring of the year A.D. 39 the Emperor Caligula stayed
at his villa at Baiae. This wealthy town stepped down in
flowered terraces to a blue gulf of sea opening upon the
Bay of Naples. Mimosa and the budded rose gleamed amid the
olive green and umber of the embracing hills. Hidden by a spur
of the shore was the busy port of Puteoli, where vessels from
Byzantium, Alexandria, and Hyspania came to discharge varied
cargoes for the hungry hordes of Rome—corn, especially corn,
carried in steady procession by the high-pooped grain ships of
Egypt. Southward glimmered the point of Capri, where the late
Emperor, Tiberius, had spent his last strange years, pursuing
dreary obscenities according to what the malicious said. The
peak of Vesuvius away to the eastward emitted its tranquil
vapour, and at its base the charming resorts of Pompeii and
Herculaneum echoed with the laughter of holiday-makers, unaware of the ashen fate preparing for them within the dreaming
cone.

But Baiae, beautiful Baiae, on "the golden shore of the goddess of love," was the sceptred queen of all resorts; exclusive,
rich in every art and device needed to appease the most
luxurious society ever known. To Baiae at appropriate seasons
flocked the fashionable, the opulent, the sophisticated, the reckless, for the diversions they have always sought—mild exercise,
gaming, eating and drinking, and sexual play. Here came the
debauched pot-belly with his horde of slaves, the wealthy poli-
tician eager to hear about what happened to be what, the reigning beauties, of course, the gay and experimental, the social
cynics—and, accompanying them, the inevitable camp-followers,
the tricksters, blackmailers, and all the upper harlotry know-

ledgeable in the very latest Egyptian and Syrian manoeuvres calculated to rekindle lubricity in the impotent. Nor were wit and talent missing; for the congregation of Baiae was stimulating to the urbane mind. The nights were warm, the water placid. Offshore, when the moon rose in aloof splendour, parties gathered on the decks of anchored barges. There the couches were drawn about low tables laden with oysters and cold game, fresh fruit and dates. The wine-cups overflowed, the torches flared, the long flutes whistled merrily. Bathing was easy; you cast off your clothes and dived in amid hilarious applause and Ovidian mockery. And all, all was sanctioned and blessed by the presence of the Imperial divinity himself, breathing the same fragrant air, grinning indulgently under the same silver moon.

That the Imperial Caligula's little lip flashed wetly in any kind of light, because he was a slavering lunatic, made no difference to Baiae. Why should it? So long as you were discreet enough to keep out of the Emperor's way—his moods being notoriously devilish—you could enjoy the social warmth of what he symbolized. Just now he was organizing a bridge of boats from the mole of Puteoli towards the beach at Baiae. Everybody was talking about it. On top of these boats there was to be laid a road, in exact replica of the Appian Way, and in due course the Emperor, oak-leaved and in full state, was to ride across it over the water. Why this absurd extravagance? Because years ago the astrologer Thrasyllus had laughed Caligula's prospects to scorn, saying that he would be no more Emperor than that he would ride on horseback across the Gulf of Baiae. Now Caligula was going to show him! Mad or not mad, there was a touch of understandable human vanity in such a plan, and perhaps Baiae approved it. For it is the singular virtue of highly experienced, but otherwise decadent, societies that they are generous towards individual fault or idiosyncrasy. Petty indictment is a Puritan vice.

Between Rome and Baiae couriers posted all through the day and night so that the Emperor and his counsellors could be kept informed of State affairs; but some activities, of course, took place at the Imperial residence at Baiae. Among these was one which, in its outcome, afforded Caligula much satisfaction. It was an embassy from the East—from Palestine. Heading what must have been an imposing retinue, calculated to impress the Court with wealth and potential majesty, there arrived in Baiae that spring the Tetrarch of Galilee and Peraea, Herod Antipas, and his wife, the beautiful Herodias. They came to ask the ruler of the world if he would confer on Antipas a kingly crown, thus raising his status from that of a tetrarch and making him the equal of his nephew Agrippa. Agrippa was an intimate and loyal friend of Caligula's who had recently been proclaimed King of Trachonitis.

Antipas was a man in his sixties. For over forty years he had administered Galilee to the satisfaction of his Roman overlords. No event, so far as he could have recalled, had given rise to any serious trouble other than the campaign of John the Baptist, which had ended eleven years earlier. Herodias had pressed for the man's death contrary to Antipas's wish, and in the end had brought it about by a piece of adroit, womanish manoeuvre in concert with her daughter Salome. But Herodias had been, and still was, the light of Antipas's eyes, the strength of his will, the source of this childless man's potency. He would never have come to petition Caligula for a crown had not Herodias insisted; for he was fearful of the Emperor. Her pleadings, cajolings, and arguments had beaten down his reluctance, and here they were —massively rich, proud, both inheritors of the blood of Herod the Great—prepared, for ambition's sake, to abase themselves at the feet of the crazy Caesar. With them, we must presume, came the Tetrarch's Ministers, chief captains, and estates to demonstrate his consequence, the regnant style of his household, and the erudition and soldierly competence with which he was surrounded.

Alas for their hopes! Another man had arrived at Baiae just after them, having speeded from Palestine by the fastest possible route. He was one Fortunatus, who brought a personal letter from King Agrippa to his beloved friend and master the Emperor. In this letter Agrippa warned Caligula that Antipas was plotting against Rome, that he had indulged in conspiracy against the late Emperor, that he was in league with the Parthians—the one enemy the Romans feared—and that he was building up a great army in Galilee, having already in his arsenals arms and equipment for seventy thousand men. False in every item, this letter reflected the cruel perfidy of Agrippa, who inherited the treacherous vein of the Herods, but hardly one of their redeeming qualities. Not only was Antipas his uncle, but Herodias was his full sister, and to their generosity and hospitality he had owed his very preservation from ruin a few years earlier.

The Tetrarch and his consort were duly summoned to the Imperial presence. It is tempting to let imagination recreate the dramatic scene, probably enacted in some open courtyard under a sapphire sky and within sound of the murmuring sea. But little detail is known of Antipas's pleading or Caesar's vituperation. Caligula accused the suppliant of every offence listed by Agrippa, condemned both husband and wife, ordered that they should be stripped of all their inheritances, dignities, and private fortunes, and that they should spend the rest of their lives in exile in Gaul. He must have worked himself into a foaming frenzy of denunciation, for it was only at the end that somebody dared to remind him that Herodias was own sister to his bosom friend Agrippa who had so loyally laid the information. The Emperor's mood changed; the other half of his poor wits came into play. He would be magnanimous, merciful, loftily superior to spite.

Herodias should have reason to be thankful that she was her brother's sister. Caligula told her that, because of this fact, he would not banish her with Antipas, and would, indeed, restore her personal fortune on condition that she lived privately and took no further part in affairs. Her reply is recorded by Josephus. If anything can be urged in mitigation of that dark and passionate creature who murdered the Baptist it is her bearing then.

"You, O Emperor," she said, "offer pardon in a magnificent manner as becomes you; but the love which I have for my husband prevents me from accepting your favour. For it is not right that I, who have been a partner in his prosperity, should forsake him in his misfortune."

Together they went into exile. Together they made their exit from the tremendous stage on which it had been their unrealized lot to play their part in time's supreme tragedy. Perhaps the only thought in the mind of Antipas as he began to understand the disastrous nature of his fall was that he would never again see his golden-veined palace or the great city of Tiberias he had built beside the Lake of Galilee. Yet others who had come with him from Tiberias may have had different and varied recollections and spoken of other things in Baiae before they returned to their distant homeland. It is not an impulsive speculation but a considerable probability that the name of Jesus Christ was first uttered on the Neapolitan shore by some member of the Galilean staff that accompanied Herod Antipas.

Tradition says there were Christians in Rome and in the district around Puteoli ten years after the Crucifixion. Certain knowledge is missing, but it was precisely ten years after the Crucifixion, which modern scholarship fixes in the spring of A.D. 29, that this fateful embassy arrived at Baiae; and when one considers the intimate links between Herod's Court and the foundation of the Christian faith the coincidence assumes significance. Antipas's own foster-brother, Manaen, who had been brought up with him, is named in the Acts of the Apostles as an original member of the Church in Antioch; presumably he had had personal experience of Jesus in Galilee. The wife of the Tetrarch's steward Chuza, as recorded by St Luke, had joined the disciples and, with her friend Mary of Magdala, had gone all the way to the foot of the cross. The man whose son was healed from Cana was a nobleman of the Court. The centurion whose servant was cured at Capernaum and who was rich enough to build a synagogue must have been a senior officer of Antipas's army commanding that important frontier region. It is a mistake to imagine that the rank of centurion was restricted to those in charge of only a hundred men. Principal centurions in the Roman army were officers of authority, on occasion even granted high trust. The centurion of Capernaum would have friends at, and was most likely familiar himself with, the Court at Tiberias.

These facts alone, stemming from the time of Christ's actual ministry, are sufficient proof that his teaching and person profoundly affected official society in Galilee. The stimulus created when the disciples came back from Jerusalem with news of the Resurrection, or in later years visited their homes, could only have deepened and widened the interest; and it is difficult to believe that, as members of the embassy to Baiae talked about affairs with their Roman counterparts, they all omitted to mention the immense religious convulsion that had taken place in their midst. We may reasonably assume that some of the Galilean leaders, themselves considered culpable, were ordered to accompany their Tetrarch into banishment, but those of lesser consequence would surely be left at liberty to regain their country.

These things happened some twenty-one years before St Paul arrived in Rome. They also happened within three years of the dismissal of Pontius Pilate from the governorship of Judaea. He had sailed for Italy, under orders to report to the Emperor Tiberius, in A.D. 36 or early 37. Before he arrived Tiberius was dead. At that point Pilate disappears from history. What treatment did he receive at Caligula's hands? Was he alive when his erstwhile neighbour and enemy, Herod Antipas, came to Baiae? Was he perhaps living in retirement not so far away in Campania? These may be idle but they are fascinating speculations.

2

The Sword of Agrippa

SHARP eyes stared from the white cliffs of Dover, following every detail of a spectacle at once majestic and frightening. In formal order, spread across a broad sweep of summer sea, came slowly shoreward the war galleys of Rome. Their sails loomed ochre and purple against the blue setting; the water foamed about their dipping oars and thrusted prows. The waists of the ships glittered as the sunshine hovered on point and blade and boss, for they were packed with soldiers. Ashore, horsemen galloped wildly along the primitive ways of Kent, rousing the kinglings. Settlements bristled with arms as the tribes prepared to meet the invaders, but the news was heavy with ill-omen. For this mighty fleet was only one of three such armadas, all setting steadily in to different points on the coast, filled with seasoned fighting men of the Empire.

It was only four years since those events at Baiae had taken place, but Caligula had been dead for two of them. During the night of terror following his assassination in Rome a soldier had pulled aside a trembling curtain to uncover the terrified Claudius, Caligula's uncle. Thereupon, in one of those fantastic episodes which mark the Roman succession, the Praetorian Guard had proclaimed him Emperor. Ungainly, timid, and diffident as he was, few could have imagined that Claudius would reign for thirteen years; yet so it turned out, and the Empire might have done a great deal worse. Even his shortcomings seemed on occasion to benefit both himself and the State. Blest with no heroic quality, he yet ardently desired to achieve heroic stature, to be imperishably linked with one of those famous Roman triumphs: it was this urge that induced him to plan the conquest of Britain.

B

Discretion being not only the better part of valour, but sometimes the secret of competence, he did not lead the expedition-
ary force himself, as Tiberius or Germanicus would have done;
he carefully chose one who seemed to be the most brilliant
strategist in the army to be its commander-in-chief. This was
Aulus Plautius, who thus found himself under orders to
accomplish a military feat that the great Julius Caesar had
botched ninety years earlier.

As he studied the nearing land of Britain from the poop of
his ship Aulus Plautius must have felt pride in his army and
confidence in the outcome of the enterprise. He had four famous
fighting legions with him—the Augusta, Gemina, Hispana, and
Valeria Victrix—some thirty thousand well-equipped veterans.
Among his legionary commanders was the extraordinarily able
Vespasian—a middle-class sort of fellow, to be sure, hardly fit
for elegant company, but what a sagacious soldier and what a
buttress to morale! It would have astounded Aulus Plautius
had he been told then that this same Vespasian would one day
be Emperor, or that he himself would find a little niche in the
history of a vast religion which was to be called Christianity.

The conquest of Britain, meticulously organized, moved reso-
lutely to schedule. There was stubborn fighting in the Medway
valley and at the approaches to the Thames, but the disunited
natives were unequal to the cleverly led legions, and in a month
or two the position in the south of the island was sufficiently
stable for the Emperor to be invited over from Gaul. Claudius,
who had been waiting for this summons, came in appropriately
conquering style with, it is said, some elephants. On British soil
—now the soil of a Roman colony—he mingled with his commanders and received from Aulus Plautius the felicitations due
to his Imperial prowess.

So Claudius Caesar stood in his new dominion. Under him
the eagles had been carried to the farthest extreme of the north-
west, to the edge of the boundless ocean. He had made the
Empire larger than it had been before, and surely his breast
warmed when he thought of its immensity: from this remote
outpost on the world's rim, across Europe and all along the
Mediterranean basin up to the Parthian frontier on the

Euphrates—the Parthian frontier beside which his faithful legions stood to arms as they did here in Britain, and near which such companions as the trusted King Agrippa of Judaea kept watch and ward also.

But while Claudius sojourned in Britain during that autumn of A.D. 43 his friend King Agrippa was forging the baleful act that was to preserve his own name from oblivion. It took place in Jerusalem a little later in the year, or perhaps early in the year following. He killed a fisherman, and thereby won the sour immortality to which his otherwise unscrupulous life would not have entitled him; for even the callous betrayal of his uncle Antipas had been without originality or distinction in the craft of cheating.

Claudius Caesar had already been an even better friend to Agrippa than the late unlamented Caligula: he had enlarged his territories and restored to him the Kingdom of Judaea, so that Agrippa now enjoyed the greater part of those lands over which his grandfather, Herod the Great, had once ruled. His state was fully regal, and he established his Court in the old Hasmonaean Palace at Jerusalem. He identified himself with the cause of Jewry as if his whole life pulsed with passionate zeal for the God of Israel and the Temple. On the principle of making the most of such opportunities as chance cast in your way—a principle by which he had managed not unsuccessfully so far—he applied himself to the task with that kind of adaptable enthusiasm which marks the typical adventurer. He would be very much a Jewish king among the Jews.

But popular feeling was not reflected in his Judaism. He was more than willingly cultivated by the aristocratic Sadducean party and the priestly caste. He was related to them by blood, especially with the family of Boethus. Moreover, their coffers were overflowing. That corruption of the great sacerdotal houses which was shortly to become notorious had already begun. They were rich and proud—conditions made possible only by tacit co-operation with Rome—and there was little love between them and the poorer classes and those genuinely pious upholders of the Law who were represented by the Pharisees.

Among Agrippa's subjects were the little group of Nazarenes

who had clung together since the crucifixion of their master fourteen years earlier. Simon Peter was at their head, and others of whom there is certain note were the disciples James and John, the sons of Zebedee, and Philip and Barnabas and John Mark. Paul too had been converted and was of their company. What had happened to other members of the original Twelve is not with certainty known. Some of those devoted women who had attached themselves to Jesus would be in frequent association with the group. That Mary, his mother, was still alive cannot be presumed, though in the course of natural events it is likely. All the indications are that she was a very young woman when he was born, and in that event she need have been no more than sixty-five or thereabouts at this time. Mary, her kinswoman, the wife of Cleophas, and Joanna, the wife of Herod Antipas's steward, would be of the same generation, Mary of Magdala being perhaps slightly younger. James, the "brother of the Lord," was a prominent member of the band and was destined to become its leader in Jerusalem. No figure stands out with more distinct clarity in the uncertain light of those distant days, convincing and splendid.

Later events confirm the belief that Jesus's family played a big part in firming the roots of Christianity; at one time there was even a dynastic movement within the community. What is known of this family? Debate has raged for centuries among theologians concerning its precise relationship to the person of Christ and his mother—a debate in which, inevitably, the doctrine of the virgin birth has been involved. Yet time, with its accumulation of objective analysis, has reduced controversy to small compass, and nothing has been established to dismay those who put their trust in the Apostle's Creed.

The first mention of the family is in the Gospel of Mark. There, after the account of Jesus's early preaching in the synagogue at Nazareth, the local people express their astonishment by saying: "Is not this man the carpenter, the son of Mary, the brother of James and Joses and of Juda and Simon? And are not his sisters here with us?" The same incident is recorded by Matthew, his version of the exclamations being: "Is not this the carpenter's son? Is not his mother called Mary? and his brethren James and Joses and Simon and Judas? And his sisters, are they not all with us?" In both accounts Mary is spoken of as the mother of Jesus, and though Matthew refers to him as the son of the carpenter, there is a clear implication that Joseph is no longer alive. Indeed, no reference to Joseph appears after this time, although Mary is frequently mentioned. The presumption of Joseph's death when Jesus was yet young is very strong, and this, while not proof, adds substance to the tradition that he was an elderly man when he became espoused to Mary, and to the further tradition that he was a widower and that the "brothers and sisters" of Jesus were in nominal fact stepbrothers and stepsisters by the carpenter's earlier marriage.

One of the most ancient Christian documents, not accepted in the canon, asserts this categorically. The *Book of James*, as it is known, purports to have been written in Jerusalem shortly after the birth of Christ. It is known to have been in circulation in the second century because writers belonging to that period refer to it. In this Greek text Joseph the widower is said to have been accompanied by his sons when he went to Bethlehem for the census; one of his sons is pictured as leading the donkey on which Mary rode. Allowance has to be made for the fictional embellishment that is a feature of such writings, but there is nothing in the manner of the *Book of James* to suggest that the previous marriage of Joseph was anything more than an accepted fact in those days: there is no presentation of a case or argument in support of a convenient theory. Moreover, James, the "brother of the Lord," is said to have been around ninety years old when he died in A.D. 62. Even placing him then in the middle eighties would make him some twenty years older than Jesus, and since Jesus was the "firstborn" of Mary the inference in relation to Joseph's earlier marriage is obvious.

Jude (named Juda and Judas in the Gospel references above), like his brother James, became a Christian. Whether he belonged to the primitive community at Jerusalem is a matter of speculation; whether these two, who are not named as being disciples or followers during the lifetime of Jesus, were converted after the Resurrection is a question for theological hypothesis; but that the family from Nazareth must have exer-

cised a powerful influence over the sect is an irresistible conclusion. From what is known of James, and from the epistle that
bears his name, it seems clear that the family were strongly
attached to the Hebrew Law and Mosaic practice. They must
have been in sympathy, both by social class and religious habit,
with the Pharisees. Deeply pious, their sense of humility in the
sight of God—quite apart from the tremendous personal experience they had undergone—would put them in stern opposition
to the worldly pomp and hardness of heart exhibited by the
Temple priesthood and the Sadducees. A like instinct and out-
look united the disciples with them. They were all Galileans
whose ways of life and northern dialect differed from the manner and speech of official Jerusalem probably as much as those
of a Yorkshire yeoman differ from those of Belgravia.

At the same time, it would be a mistake to imagine these
remarkable men as being illiterate and vulgarly rustic. The Acts
describe Peter and John as "unlearned and ignorant," but this
is strictly in relation to the appearance they had just made
before the High Priest and elders of the Sanhedrin—an assembly in which the most notable scholars of Israel would have
been numbered. The inspiration burning within the Galilean
disciples lent them obvious eloquence and authority, but it was
superimposed on minds that were not originally bereft of
enlightenment.

Men like Peter and the sons of Zebedee would have been
taught some writing, the reading of the Scriptures, and elementary numbers at the synagogue schools of Capernaum or
Bethsaida—the kind of education Jesus himself must have
received at Nazareth. They would almost certainly know a
passable amount of Greek, or at least the *koine*, for a lot of
Greek was spoken in and around Galilee. These men did not
spring from the lowest orders. They were hard-working *bourgeois* tradesmen, living in modest comfort. In Peter's house at
Capernaum, for example, Jesus had stayed when Peter himself,
his wife, and his wife's mother were also present. Zebedee seems
to have conducted quite a considerable fishing business in which
his sons, James and John, helped him. They had "hired servants"—paid employees—also to man the boats, and the wife

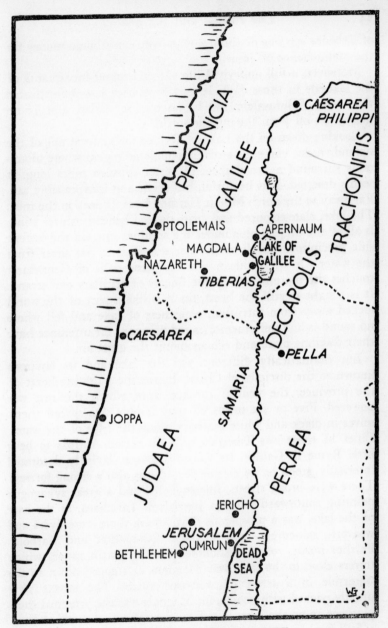

PALESTINE IN THE FIRST CENTURY

of Zebedee was one of those women who contributed money for the maintenance of Jesus.

Moreover, a full and vivid life surged around inhabitants of the lakeside in those days. It may have been less sophisticated than that of Jerusalem, but it was intense, varied, and by no means cut off from the outside world.

Looking down on the Lake of Galilee to-day from one of the upland tracks, you see a sparsely populated region where mountains surround a broad sheet of water thirteen miles long. It seems deserted. It is beautiful, but silent and inexpressibly sad Far away to the north Mount Hermon loses its peak in the mist. The lake, slate-coloured and foam-dashed beneath winter wind. is all of the deepest blue under the summer sun. On the eastern side precipitous purple-brown steeps appear to rise sheer from the water. On the Galilean side the green oasis of Gennesaret touches the margin with gentle fingers of fritillary and strand. It is a sight to still the heart, for it is like a part of the world locked away from intrusion; a fastness of lake and fell where no sound is and only memories too poignant for utterance have their dwelling-place and echoes haunt the quiet air.

But dramatically different was the lake and its environs known to the disciples of Christ. It was the pulsating heart of the province, the central furnace from which the rest was powered. Five or six towns of considerable size spread themselves in black and white masonry along the edge of the water Chief of these was Tiberias, built by Herod Antipas to be a little Rome in Galilee. Its splendid palace, lavishly decorated internally, stood on an eminence and was also a strong fortress There were broad streets, fine markets, and a great synagogue pointing southward towards Jerusalem. Tarichaea, at the base of the lake, was a prosperous town where there were dyers and weavers, salt-curers, and a large fish-market and harbour. Farther north, round a shoulder of the Hattin range, which towers close to the lake, was Magdala. It stepped down to the waterside in a series of well-used roads. The streets were usually packed with people, for Magdala was the principal shopping centre on the lake.

Still farther north, near Capernaum, ran the mightiest highway of the area—the Way of the Sea, the Damascus road. All that passed southward, to Egypt and Judaea, and westward, to Tyre, Ptolemais, Athens, and Rome, moved along it—caravans of camels and asses laden with the merchandise of Arabia, Armenia, and the Persian Gulf; mule trains from Syria; groups of travellers tramping with staff and pack; guarded ladies borne at speed in palanquins; pilgrims heading for Jerusalem; itinerant craftsmen, poorly sandalled and wearing sackcloth, pushing whetstone or barrow; wandering Rabbis, pedlars of dubious goods. A perpetual haze of dust hung over the two sections of the route—the one which came down apparently over the hill and the other which emerged from the streets of Capernaum. A perpetual hoarseness of voices, mingling with the cracking of whips, the tinkle of bells, and the crying of animals, marked its courses. Capernaum itself stretched for a distance about the north-western bend of the lake. It was loud with movement, with the creaking of cart and bale, and up the side streets probably a large population was crowded in houses and tenements.

This, then, was the native region whence the Apostles, now in Jerusalem, had come. Two of them, together with Paul of Tarsus, were to win a supremacy in fame that places them above the reach of all other men of renown. They were Peter and John. Already these two, who were constantly in each other's company, had been imprisoned and flogged for their activities. Their healing and preaching, of course, were regarded by the hierarchical priesthood as Jewish heresies rather than foundations for a new faith: it is to be borne in mind that for many years, both in Asia and Europe, Christianity was conceived as a branch of Judaism.

Short missionary journeys into adjacent districts had already begun; in these Peter, John, Philip, Barnabas, and Paul had taken part. Their followers increased rapidly, and a number of Rabbis joined them, as well as Jews from various parts of the Graeco-Roman world who came to make their pilgrimages to Jerusalem. Contemplating the dramatic growth of this heretical society, the Sadducees and the Temple clique, headed by the High Priest Annas, were increasingly alarmed, and they invoked the aid of the king. Only too willing to fall in with the wishes of established orthodoxy, Agrippa decided to take action.

James, the elder son of Zebedee, was quickly secured. He must have been brought before some sort of tribunal, possibly before Agrippa himself, for he was condemned and put to death. Beheading would appear to have been the means by which the last Herodian monarch spilt the first blood of a disciple, for, we are told, "he killed James, the brother of John, with the sword."

The failure of his soldiers speedily to lay hands on other leaders of the sect suggests that they had gone to ground—or maybe were dispersed on missions about Palestine—for the High Priest and his associates expressed much satisfaction over the death of James, and Agrippa was eager to give further evidence of his devotion to the State religion. But presently a prize worth waiting for fell into his power. This was Simon Peter himself, the chief of the Nazarenes, the cornerstone of the Church-to-be. Peter was arrested in the Passover season of A.D. 44. Perhaps he had decided to show himself boldly in Jerusalem as the anniversary of the Resurrection drew near: it would be an impulsive move typical of the man. He was thrust into prison, Agrippa's intention being to display him captive around Eastertide, thus making a mock of the Christians before committing him to the same fate as James.

Had Agrippa been able to wreak his bloody vengeance on this great man the history of Christianity would have been different, but Providence decreed that it should not be. Peter escaped from his jailers. On some dark and chilly night just after Easter —a night when tense Roman sentries amid the forests of hostile Britain watched every sullen glade—Peter the disciple slipped furtively through the narrow streets of Jerusalem, pausing in the shadows to listen for pursuers, until he found his way to the house where John Mark's mother lived. He knocked on the outer gate, no doubt discreetly at first so as not to arouse the neighbourhood. One of those inside, a girl named Rhoda, was sent to listen. She asked who it was, and when Peter replied she recognized his voice. She ran to tell the rest of the company, leaving the unfortunate man in the street.

Time was pressing; Peter must somehow get out of the way

of the king's soldiers. He knocked harder. Meantime, when those in the house heard Rhoda exclaiming that Peter was outside they told her she was mad and must have seen his spirit, for they had become resigned to his death. However, as he hammered away in demonstration of a most unspiritlike condition, they eventually opened the gate to discover him. There was little time for congratulation or expression of joy. He gave them terse instructions. They must tell James—that is, James, the stepbrother of Jesus—and the rest of the Nazarenes what had happened. Then, no doubt after hastily providing himself with food and drink, "he departed and went into another place."

This, the most important 'escape story' of all, rings true to human experience in every line of those passages written by Luke in The Acts. The secret, anxious gathering at the home of Mark's mother—a woman probably unsuspected by the authorities—Rhoda's tremulous inquiry of the one who knocked—her reluctance to open the gate in spite of her certainty that Peter was there—the urgency with which he passed on his important message to James—the mystery of his destination when he left them—all this has an atmosphere similar to those which have brooded, thunder-charged, over many an underground movement in modern times. Detail convinces, even to the girl's identity. Who was Rhoda and what became of her? Did ever a fleeting minor character—a name, a swift excited running, a pair of dark Jewish eyes, round with astonishment—attain such fadeless remembrance?

Where Peter went to outwit Agrippa's spies is not known. The king's wrath descended on the four quarternions of soldiers who had let their prisoner elude them; they were put to death. It is unlikely that Peter travelled any great distance, for he was back in Jerusalem within measurable time, taking part in a council that was called to discuss whether uncircumcised Gentiles could be admitted to the Church. Both he and James voiced the case for tolerance, and it prevailed.

Herod Agrippa, having consolidated his position with the Sadducees by killing Zebedee's son and openly persecuting the Nazarene sect, did not long enjoy his kingdom. At Caesarea, where he moved from Jerusalem shortly after Peter's escape,

he summoned before him a deputation of Tyrians to consider
an offence of which he regarded their city-state to be guilty.
He was clad in all his majesty and surrounded by the impressive
vestments of his Court. Amid this pomp he delivered an oration
that caused flatterers to say he was not human, but divine.
They spoke too soon, for suddenly, unlike a god, he fell dying
from his throne. They said he was "eaten of worms," but it is
more likely that he was smitten by coronary thrombosis and
that his agonized last minutes suggested something was gnawing
his vitals. Josephus describes his end in terms that fully sub-
stantiate the New Testament account.

Agrippa left a son who in due course became Agrippa II of
Judaea; but he was not allowed to succeed to kingly power. The
Emperor decided that it was unwise to perpetuate the new-
Herodian line. He restored the system of Augustus and Tiberius
under which Judaea was administered by a Roman governor
and policed by Roman auxiliary forces. The young Agrippa
became a puppet monarch whose authority was limited to the
surveillance of the Temple and of Jewish social affairs.

He had two sisters, each of whom embodied a personality
beside which that of their brother paled. Both were beautiful
and passionate—an inheritance among Herodian women that
had bewitched men for three generations. The elder, Berenice,
was cruelly envious of the surpassing loveliness of Drusilla, her
sister, who when she grew up was renowned as the most
entrancing woman of her time. Each of them was to fill a rôle
in history; each was to play a transient part in the unfolding
drama of Christianity.

3

The Road and the Statue

THE death of Agrippa I freed the Nazarenes from persecution. It was not possible for the Sanhedrin to oppress them now that direct Roman authority had been reimposed. The High Priest and his friends had their wings clipped once the new procurator arrived in Caesarea and an Imperial garrison took over the Tower of Antonia in Jerusalem. By every means at their command they must have manoeuvred against the Nazarene heresy, but they dare not use physical force upon its teachers and proselytes—at least, not openly. The years that followed saw the great missionary journeys of Paul and Barnabas and Mark and the establishment of the Church in Asia—at Antioch of Syria and Ephesus and Pergamos and Smyrna. Its adherents multiplied quickly, and they now called themselves Christians.

For the activities of Peter and John in the period immediately after Agrippa's death there is no written authority. Even tradition does not gather round the figure of John until later, when it becomes significant and unites with what is known of his old age. In the case of Peter it points to his having made journeys into parts of Asia: he may well have gone farther north than Paul, into the provinces of Cappadocia and Pontus towards the Black Sea; but nothing is known with certainty. Out of much lore it is impossible to reach any conclusions other than the obvious ones that Peter had no Luke to put down an account of his travels and was less given to writing letters than Paul. He was, of course, not so highly literate a man. Nevertheless, the one epistle that may reasonably be ascribed to his inspiration (Peter I), though it was written many years later, is addressed to the people of those distant Asian provinces with which his name is otherwise linked, and may be taken as a degree of confirmation that he had earlier visited them.

Paul's travels are described in such detail in The Acts and are featured in so many biographies that it is unnecessary to pursue them here. But it must have been in the period of his first journey through southern Asia Minor, about A.D. 49–50, that the seeds of two notable legends were sown. These legends flowered in the rich soil of primitive Christian imagination, and spread their branches far into the air of romance; but when their lushest blooms are plucked and the gilded husk is torn from their stems there is to be found at the source of each a germ of authentic, seminal truth.

The story of Paul and Thekla has been preserved in several versions; it is written in Greek, Latin, Arabic, and Slavonic. Briefly, it tells how, on Paul's visit to Iconium, the Phrygian city, the daughter of a wealthy household, Thekla, came under the spell of his preaching. When the local authorities imprisoned him she visited him in jail, bribing his guards with her dressing-table jewellery. Later she abandoned her unhappy sweetheart in order to follow Paul to Antioch, in Pisidia. In that city, falling foul of Alexander, the president of a festival that was just beginning, she was condemned to be exhibited in the amphitheatre and devoured by wild beasts. But when she was cast into the ring, clad only in the customary brief girdle, the beasts refused to eat her. Indeed, a lioness took her part and killed a bear and a lion in her defence; and further miracles now began to multiply while the devilry of her persecutors became so sadistic that a lady in the audience, called Queen Tryphaena, fainted. This incident worried the festival officials very much, for the fainted lady, they said, was a relative of the Emperor; so they released Thekla and let her go to Tryphaena's house. After this Thekla's activities develop into the fabulous, sacrificial, and mystic.

Variations and romantic adornments to this story flowed from busy pens over the centuries, but it was not until comparatively recent times that, as a result of work by men like Mommsen, Von Gutschmid, and Sir W. M. Ramsay, the historical bases of the legend have been indicated. Queen Tryphaena, long regarded as being as fictitious as Titania, is now known to have been a real person, the mother of a King of Pontus who began his reign in A.D. 37. She was a second cousin of Claudius Caesar; therefore most certainly related to the Emperor and not a lady whose sensibilities could be affronted with equanimity by a provincial games-master.

But there is a further intriguing aspect of this story on which Professor Ramsay was able to throw new light. Embedded in its several variants is a celebrated description of St Paul. It occurs at a point in the narrative where a citizen of Iconium named Onesiphorus goes to meet the Apostle on his way from Antioch and stands on the "Royal Road to Lystra." He sees Paul approaching—a small, strongly built man, bald, bow-legged, with meeting eyebrows and a large nose.

This reference to a "Royal Road" seemed to point to the second century, when such highways were known to be in exist-ence, and, coupled with other suggestive features, lent force to the theory that the whole legend stemmed from that compara-tively late date. In 1884, however, there was found in the same region a milestone announcing that the "Royal Road" on which it once stood was constructed by "the Emperor Caesar Augustus by care of his lieutenant Cornelius Aquila." Such roads, there-fore, existed in Pisidia even before the time of St Paul, and Ramsay indicates the very side-turning which led to Iconium, drawing the conclusion that the elemental features of the Thekla story had their source in somebody with precise geo-graphic and historic knowledge.[1] Thekla must have been a real person who had contact with Paul and the queen dowager of an adjacent realm. Moreover, with this knowledge is it not possible to place more credence than otherwise on the account of Paul's appearance, especially in view of its unflattering nature? A fiction-writer eager to invest the Apostle with wond-rous attributes would hardly have given him bow legs.

Here is an example of what relentless probing can uncover even after nearly two thousand years have gone by. The tale of Thekla and Paul remains a decorative romance, but breathing behind it are genuine human beings, moving about in a real

[1] See *The Church in the Roman Empire*, by W. M. Ramsay (Hodder and Stoughton).

world, and from them it derived its impulse. It was not, at its beginning, summoned out of thin air by an ardent convert or literary monk.

The other legend which may be given its germinal setting in this period, and is also vested in fact, is that of Veronica. She appears in a great amount of tradition, usually associated with a picture or representation of Christ. One story is that she was a niece of Herod the Great and offered her veil as a *sudarium* to Jesus on his way to crucifixion, whereupon his features were engraven on the linen. Face-cloths from the catacombs painted with supposed portraits of Christ were called 'veronicas,' and miraculous power was attributed to them. The woman to whom this name is given in the legend is identified with the one who was cured by Jesus as recounted in the Gospel of Matthew (Chapter ix):

> And behold, a woman which was diseased with an issue of blood twelve years came behind him and touched the hem of his garment; for she said within herself, If I may but touch his garment I shall be whole. But Jesus turned him about and when he saw her he said, Daughter, be of good comfort; thy faith hath made thee whole. And the woman was made whole from that hour.

In the fourth-century *Acts of Pilate* Veronica is introduced into the account of the trial of Christ, where she cries out testifying to the miracle that had been worked in her. Like the other tales, this is utterly fanciful. All are, in fact, late traditions. But their source is genuine enough; it comes from one of the most dramatic paragraphs in the works of Eusebius. Eusebius, who was appointed Bishop of Caesarea in A.D. 313, was by far the most important and reliable historian of the ancient Church. To his habit of quotation still earlier writers owe their very preservation, for their original works in many cases are lost. Describing the other Caesarea—Caesarea Philippi, that former capital of the Tetrarch of Trachonitis, lying at the foot of Mount Hermon, beyond Galilee's northern frontier—Eusebius records this, in about the year A.D. 325:

> They say that she who had an issue of blood and who, as we learn from the sacred Gospels, found at the hands of our Saviour

relief from her affliction, came from this place, and that her house was pointed out in the city, and that marvellous memorials of the kindness which the Saviour had wrought upon her remained. For (they said) there stood on a lofty stone at the gates of her house a brazen figure in relief of a woman, bending on her knee and stretching forth her hands like a suppliant, while opposite to this there was another of the same material, an upright figure of a man, clothed in comely fashion in a double cloak and stretching out his hand to the woman. At his feet on the monument itself a strange species of herb was growing which climbed up to the border of the double cloak of brass, and acted as an antidote to all kinds of diseases. This statue, they said, bore the likeness of Jesus. And it was in existence even to our day, so that we saw it with our own eyes when we stayed in the city.

It is, of course, the last sentence in this passage that fires the imagination. Eusebius—the dependable, the scholarly, the shrewd discarder of the dubious—had seen these statues, or one of them, with his own eyes, not, it would appear, in their original position, but presumably in some other place at Caesarea Philippi. If their carving and erection had been carried out within ten years of Christ's ministry on the instructions of the grateful woman herself—and that is a rational assumption—they would have been antique objects some 280 years later. Had they been put up after her death, or by the earliest Christian community there, they would still have been venerable works. People in the city who took an interest in old landmarks—and where is the town that does not possess such zealots?—must have taken what remained of the statues for safe-keeping, either to the church or to some equivalent of a modern museum; and there the renowned Bishop of Caesarea must have examined them when he toured the outer regions of Palestine. It is easy to understand how the legends developed which associated Veronica with effigies and portraits of Jesus, but that is the least significant element in this report by Eusebius. He goes on to explain that among the Gentiles "the ancients" were accustomed to pay tribute in this way to those who had been their saviours or deliverers. Plainly he knew the statues to be very old, and he implies that Veronica herself had caused them to be set up.

She cannot have been a Jewess, for no Jewess would have

c

dared to break the Mosaic Law by making a "graven image."
If she did commission the sculpture herself she must have been
affluent, a likelihood supported by the possession of gates impressive enough to be embellished in this way. The whole
episode is surrounded with realistic circumstance: the woman,
her home, and her gratitude, lifted out of what is to us the
supernatural context of the Gospel, assume a convincing shape
and meaning, and belong to the kind of world with which we
are familiar.

During the period of Christ's ministry in Galilee and for some
five or six years after the Crucifixion Caesarea Philippi was the
administrative capital of Herod Philip, the Tetrarch of
Trachonitis, half-brother of Antipas. He was a kindly, unambi-
tious man, celebrated for even-handed justice and the diligence
with which he cultivated his mixed and scattered peoples. Late
in life he married the dancing Salome, who had achieved
notoriety by asking for the head of John the Baptist at Antipas's
feast. Philip must have been around fifty years old, and Salome
no more than twenty, when this odd wedding was celebrated.
They lived in the palace at Caesarea Philippi until his death in
A.D. 34. Were they ever acquainted with that woman of substance, their subject, who had been healed by Jesus and planned
the striking effigies outside her house in the city?

How long Salome remained in Caesarea Philippi during her
widowhood is unknown. Since she married again, this time a
young kinsman, Aristobulus, the likelihood is that she did not
waste too many of her summered years unaccompanied in bed.
But it was another wedding that led to the next point of contact between the Herodians and the Christians.

A year or two after Paul, Barnabas, and Mark had sailed from
Cyprus to the Asian mainland at the outset of their missions
another ship carried a new governor of Judaea across the
Mediterranean from Rome to Palestine. His name was Felix. As
a young man Felix could never, even in his most abandoned
dreams, have foreseen that he would some day hold such an
important position of trust, for he came of a slave family and
had neither capacity nor acquired culture. What he did possess
was a remarkable brother, Pallas—one of those persons who

concentrate their natural dynamism into a single amoral purpose. Pallas the freedman wanted power. Through a mixture of unctuous toadyism and excellent, timely advice he became the Emperor's most intimate confidant. He amassed a fortune that was fabulous even in the Rome of those fabulous days, by what means nobody now knows. His pervasive power extended to awesome proportions. Men from the highest official and social stations waited patiently in the reception rooms of Pallas the freedman.

By his own qualities Felix would hardly have made a mark beyond whatever village claimed his nativity; but, being the brother of this golden Pallas, a job had to be found for him, so he was sent to Caesarea by Claudius to administer the province of Judaea and keep a watchful eye on the young king, Agrippa II.

Hard and stubborn though they were, the men who in years gone by had served as Roman governors in Palestine were men of character and ability. Annius Rufus, Valerius Gratus, Pontius Pilate—each in turn, while exercising that inflexible, cruelty-stained authority that was traditional in the Roman service, had, according to his lights, sought to forward the interests of the province and its inhabitants. A decaying standard was pioneered by Felix. He was the first of a series of governors whose self-indulgence, arrogance, and morbid incapacity led in no small measure to those catastrophes that were to come upon Israel in general and Jerusalem in particular. Backed by the power behind the throne in the person of his brother, profligate and sensual in his own life, inheriting no code but that of self-interest, not consumed by even the meanest of ambitions, Felix regarded his appointment merely as a means to the gratification of whatever whim of indulgence happened to possess him. In his colony he had Imperial authority; in his mind simmered nothing of Imperial responsibility.

Within a short time of his arrival in Judaea the new governor met Drusilla, Agrippa's bewitching younger sister. She was then, though only sixteen, married to Azizus, King of Emesa; but, since her excelling loveliness enraptured him, Felix instantly resolved that she should be his wife. Was he not the master of Judaea? A divorce from his majesty of Emesa presented no difficulty; it should be done. Nevertheless, it seems that Felix's aggressive wooing had to be reinforced by other arts, for he called in the services of a Cypriot magician. Amid the mumbo-jumbo which this gentleman practised on the girl was the cogent argument that, as Rome's delegate and as Pallas's brother, Felix had a great deal more to offer than a secondary kingling like Azizus. She, being a Herod, was not indifferent to the main chance. She consented, became the third wife of Felix, and presently in the governor's residence at Caesarea bore him a son.

This little boy came into the world most probably in the very year when the Emperor Claudius made his poisoned exit, A.D. 54. He would have been a toddler of about four when the most notable event occurred in the life of his beautiful young mother. At the time she can hardly have appreciated a fragment of its consequence, though it may well be that in later years she recalled it with deepening interest.

St Paul returned to Jerusalem from Europe and Ephesus. While in the Temple courts he was accused by Jews who had known his activities in Asia of preaching heresy, and the crowd closed in on him murderously. Roman soldiers from the adjacent Tower of Antonia, the headquarters of the garrison, hastened to stop the brawl and to rescue him, and after he had been examined by their commandant, Claudius Lysias, and discovered to be a Roman citizen, he was sent to Caesarea under a strong guard of cavalry and infantry. There he was brought before Felix, the governor, who remanded him in the custody of a centurion, only to summon him to a private audience a few days later.

This time the governor was accompanied by his wife, Drusilla, apparently because she was a Jewess familiar with the religious sects of the land. In her presence the prisoner was asked to explain the Christian faith.

Thus the great Apostle stood before the brutish Felix and the most celebrated beauty of the East. Paul was a man of fifty now; the marks of his travels and sufferings were on him, for he had been beaten and shipwrecked, imprisoned and hounded. Under scorching sun and amid upland snowy ways, often in remote and perilous regions, he had preached the Gospel for nearly ten years. His unprepossessing, bow-legged figure must have been in dramatic contrast with the dazzling young woman who put questions to him that day in Caesarea. What they said is not recorded, only that as Paul "reasoned of righteousness, temperance, and the judgment to come, Felix trembled." That is not surprising.

The Apostle was again remanded, and, in fact, was kept under light detention in the city for two years, Felix hoping to receive some ransom for him. They met and talked again; maybe Drusilla was with them on these other occasions. But meantime in Rome one whose name looms terribly in the annals of Christianity was consolidating his position as Emperor. The purple had fallen on Nero.

4

The Capital of the World

COLUMNS, colonnades, and temples stood nobly about the heart of Rome; the sunshine spilt gold upon its marbled pavements and warmed the fluttering white togas of its lawyers and senators on the Forum steps. But this was not the Rome in which the masses passed their noisome, unlettered lives. They were packed in the semi-darkness of the poorer regions.

All day long the jumbled narrow streets—hardly more than alleys between blank-walled apartment houses—were loud with the cries of vendors and the clatter of workmen. The butcher, the baker, the barber, and the fuller displayed their wares, or carried on their activities, beside the shadowed walls. Refuse and ordure stank; fevers were rampant. Over a million men, women, and children were herded there, most of them living a slum tenement life.

By night the noise and the confusion were even worse. For it had been decreed in earlier times that, because of congestion, wheeled vehicles should be permitted to pass through the streets only after sundown. All the merchandise necessary to the existence of the world's capital had to be brought in or taken out at night. A creaking, lumbering procession of carts moved up and down the steep ways, with the concomitant cursing of drivers and stamping of horses, while in foetid rooms only a few yards above them people tried to sleep. Rome and insomnia were notoriously synonymous.

No light illumined the streets at night. Not a lamp, not a candle, pierced the darkness. Honest citizens hastened to their homes and shut themselves in because the passages were infested with robbers and drunken revellers. The watch was ineffective and subject to bribery; and in its wisdom it did not interfere too much with the sport of the rich. For young bloods from the noble and wealthy houses of Rome found it a hilarious diversion to storm through their 'East End,' often accompanied by well-armed servants, beating up passers-by and raping their women-folk. Woe betide those who offered unseemly resistance! They were sabred and left to die.

Darkness, disease, poverty, and crime—these haunted the courses of the Roman mob. By way of compensation they had something like a hundred holidays a year, when in their scores of thousands they streamed to the races and the games. The Roman gods looked down on it all—Apollo, Juno, Jupiter, Minerva, Ceres, and the rest of them—but the gods had grown pretty meaningless except to love-sick girls or as patrons of festivals. The only effective god was the Emperor himself. He could create and he could destroy. If he felt so disposed he scattered gifts to his people. If they offended him he had them killed or transported. That was being a real god. Caesar was indeed divine: the rest did not truly matter. One paid lip-service to them, of course, and sometimes said one's prayers with fervour during thunderstorms or earth tremors. Even so, they were gods in twilight.

Caesar alone was almighty, and Caesar was now Nero Claudius, a fat, spotty-faced, fair-haired, sulky-mouthed very young man whose main personal preoccupations were to escape from the dominance of his baleful mother, Agrippina, and to find some one more delicious in the lists of love than his frigid teen-age wife, Octavia, who had been foisted on him. In these domestic afflictions his divinity did not seem to help him much, but the mob were not to know that. They delighted in him; he was so young and was said to have a jolly disposition, and he had certainly begun his reign with a most temperate and loving proclamation.

But that proclamation had not been devised by Nero himself. The most illustrious pen of the age, the steel-worded, astringent pen of Lucius Annaeus Seneca, had composed it. At this time in his late fifties, the great philosopher and rhetorician was Nero's tutor and adviser. Seneca was a paradoxical character.

His mind was austere, his meditations profound, yet he had a worldly wisdom uncommon among scholars. A touch of pity leavened his less pungent satires, and while he exhibited the frailty of avarice and grew conceited in proportion as he dictated the literary taste of the town, thereby incurring censure from the unco guid, he bore himself nobly. On the young Emperor his influence was beneficial and in the interest of the State; but more than any other man he understood his pupil and knew the awful potential within that flabby and seemingly complacent exterior.

How far should Nero be humoured lest his formidable temper broke out? How far should he be allowed to satiate himself with pleasure lest repression caused him to discover the uses of venom? These, Seneca knew well, were questions of prime importance. In Agrippina, the Emperor's mother, he saw danger. She was resolved to rule through her son, an assertion of misconceived authority that could only lead to violent reaction when the son's smouldering resentment leapt into flame. Therefore Seneca encouraged those traits in the Emperor that would help to free him from her toils.

The young man wanted a mistress; that would be a sensible way of quenching his lust and occupying his attention. His prominent grey eyes had been seen to roam imaginatively about the exquisite face and figure of Acte, a slave-girl from Asia, and the philosopher did not allow any asceticism of mind to oppose an intrigue. It could do no harm, for the girl was quiet, tender, discreet, and loyal, and it would be a timely challenge to Agrippina's possessiveness.

One of Nero's town-chasing friends, Marcus Salvius Otho, was an accomplice in this affair. An engaging rake who belonged to a consular family, Otho, had he lived to-day, would have been regularly leading the gossip columns of the newspapers— popular in café society, a frequenter of shadier resorts, a gambler, and tough. He was destined to wear the purple for a fleeting month or two later in the century, but at this time— A.D. 55—he was enjoying all the diversions the Imperial city could offer a rich gallant in his early twenties. A son of one of the Emperor's freedmen helped him in the negotiations with

Acte, and a certain Annaeus Serenus, an intimate of Seneca's, provided the blind by pretending that he himself was Acte's lover when he carried Nero's gifts to her. His name confirms a suspicion that the girl was originally in the household of the Annaea family—that is, Seneca's family.

At this point the mystery both of Acte's personal life and the nature of her setting begins. From memorials of name and association there is a belief that the Annaea numbered among their friends members of the first Christian group in Rome. Every reference to Acte herself, and what is known of her later conduct, confirm that she was humble, gentle, and constant. She shines like a little cleanly candle against a lurid and obscure background, as if she had been at least familiar with a purer air. She was not a slave of the lowest rank, for she had an under-slave, or *vicarius*, to do her bidding, and it is obvious that a certain elegance attached to her.

That modesty and a tranquil, affectionate disposition should have lent themselves to Nero's desires might be accounted for either by Acte's being simple or by the Emperor's power of compulsion; but the fact is otherwise and more remarkable. The girl loved him dearly. Her subsequent history proves this beyond challenge. Alone of all those who had been flattered to know him, or had fawned on him in his glory, and in spite of having long been rejected, she followed him to the grave.

When the liaison came to the ears of Agrippina she expressed her fury and contempt in withering terms. "A servant-girl is to be a mother's rival!" she cried; but she had to suffer the importation of the girl, now a freedwoman with the name Claudia Acte, into the Imperial household. To ease the further transition by which the Emperor's mistress was completely emancipated from taint of serfdom a pedigree was prepared, and though this was in its details a concoction, it throws light on her place of origin. Witnesses testified that she was of the royal house of Attalus, a family that long ruled from the city of Pergamos, in Asia Minor, before they bequeathed their dominions to Rome. Without accepting such a convenient document as true, it is reasonable to believe that Claudia Acte came from Pergamos or its neighbourhood; and again the brush of the

Christian *pallium* murmurs about her associations, for one of the earliest Christian churches was established at Pergamos, and between it and the faithful in Rome there was constant intercourse.

The mob in its unwashed skin and sweaty shirt being always righteous, it is unlikely that Nero appeared in public with Acte; his poor little wife, Octavia, would be suffered on such occasions. But Roman society knew all about the affair. The eighteen-year-old Emperor and his seventeen-year-old paramour were subjects of the greatest interest and topical allusion over the fruit and wine. Graver people, pondering how the young monarch would evolve and what might be the outcome of Agrippina's jealousy, debated it in reference to the general welfare. They took comfort in the knowledge that the wise Seneca retained Nero's goodwill and watched his behaviour and his interest closely. So long as that lofty and experienced mind prevailed things would not get out of hand.

Seneca moved among the senatorial and military dignitaries as well as among the orators and lawyers; doubtless some of them discussed palace affairs with him discreetly. These may well have included the venerated Aulus Plautius, the general who had conquered Britain and had now retired in Rome after having governed the colony for some years from Colchester. He lived quietly with his wife, Pomponia Graecina, a lady of noble rank and a remarkable personality in the city. During the reign of Claudius Caesar she had spent much of her time at the palace, but on the death of Julia, Tiberius's granddaughter, to whom she was passionately devoted, she had changed her mode of life. Solemnity governed her dress and her deportment. People said she had gone into perpetual mourning for her friend, yet she was not aloof and her bearing won a certain deepening admiration. Her secret was presently to be investigated in an affair that was a tonic for gossiping tongues.

Meanwhile, under the watchful eyes of Seneca, the young Emperor tried to devote himself to his duties; but as he flexed the limbs of absolute power and, from high windows, looked across his seething capital, delusions of a grandeur beyond even this flickered in his unhealthy mind. Sometimes he broke out in impetuous sprees. Like Otho and the bloods, he took to roaming the streets at night, waylaying passers-by. On one occasion, meeting more than he had bargained for, he was given a good hiding, whereupon he ordered gladiators to accompany him. He laid plans for a vast new amphitheatre in the Field of Mars; he dreamed about an immense new palace that would be called the House of Gold, with colonnades stretching three miles and gardens and parklands extending from the Palatine Hill to the Esquiline. Much of his time was spent in designing novel shows and games. Popular applause enraptured him: the more he fed the mob with entertainment the more tumultuously, of course, they hailed his beneficence. He began to write verses in feeble imitation of Seneca's rhetoric. Perhaps there was some envy of his tutor's fame—but how could an ageing pedagogue compete with empurpled genius? Time and the gods were on his side. And, marvellously, Acte loved him.

If judgment pauses before condemning Nero as an unmitigated monster it is partly because of this. Claudia Acte loved him, and she was both upright and sane. She continued to love him when the whole world had become sickened by his vileness and vanity and when even in the nostrils of hardened soldiers his name reeked repellently. To them cruelty was commonplace, but its refinements were not, while obscenity should have its limits. There can be but one reason for Acte's devotion—that she perceived not only Nero's mental derangement, but that it reduced his instincts and imaginings to those of a sickly child. Perhaps in the intimacy of their first embraces, when he was still very much afraid of his mother, he drew compassion from her as an infant might have drawn milk from her breast. Hers was a maternal love for one whose most appalling actions she believed to be only the posturings of a deficient popinjay, an immature swashbuckler, a vain mountebank, and therefore did not imply moral responsibility. Though so many suffered at his behest and his hands befouled what they touched, he was to her but a pitiable undeveloped clown-child, conceitedly asserting that he was godlike. There must have been within him some attractive streak—some point of human confession and weakness—that she had glimpsed before it was frozen up. She alone

knew, only she understood, what accounted for the paradox
whereby, in spite of his criminal enormities, he appears as a
buffoon, investing with an atmosphere of grotesque comedy
even the incandescent tragedy over which he presided.

Yet up to now nothing in Nero's conduct or expression raised
any real disquiet. Youth must be allowed to pursue its follies.
In the spring of A.D. 57 long processions of carts brought timber
to the Field of Mars and workmen raised day-long clamour with
adze and axe and hammer, building the Emperor's new amphitheatre. Here was a fresh topic for the town that must have
engaged not only the anticipatory mob, for whose entertainment
it was intended, but the politer elements, among whom moved
Gaius Petronius, the witty, urbane, and debauched cynic, Court
jester to the Emperor.

Little in Rome escaped Petronius's life-loving eyes. To him the
filthy lower ways by the Tiber were, by sight at least, almost as
familiar as the villas about the Capitoline. The bearded Jew
chasing his squawky hen down a dungy yard was equally a part
of the play with the epicure sipping his wine in a fountained
atrium. Indeed, the Jews were becoming quite an influence in
the city, as anybody who enjoyed the company of fashionable
women could affirm. It was now *the* thing for a woman of taste
to have her pet Jew and improve her mind by the study of his
ancient lore. Some even professed to have become converted to
the Jewish religion and to have found in it unutterable solace
for their exhausted spirits. Maybe this was merely a matter of
boredom discovering a novelty. That the women and not the
men succumbed to its attractions was due, said the satirical, to
the fact that they did not have to undergo that awful business
of circumcision.

A strange people, the Hebrews, to be found anywhere where
there was trade to be done or money to be made, yet dwelling
apart in their Oriental mysticism and worshipping their in-
visible God with melancholy ritual. There must have been then
several thousand of them in Rome, living in their own quarter
close to their synagogues and slaughter-houses. It was also said
that a new sect had established itself among them (though it
was not in favour with their priests), and that this sect had a

particular appeal to Gentile women because it was devoted to the deification of love and was accompanied by secret rites of an appropriately orgiastic nature. Its adherents used terms of endearment on meeting, exchanged kisses, ate a sacred meal behind closed doors, and, it was alleged, when the lights had been put out, indulged in promiscuous sexual intercourse on the banquet couches.

Suddenly the town rang with speculation about these things. A storm broke on the head of the famous general, Aulus Plautius. His wife, Pomponia Graecina, was accused by the authorities of being subject to "a foreign superstition," and, according to custom, her husband and his family were ordered to investigate the charge. It must have been a bewildering blow to the dignified soldier when he received the Senate's indictment. What a nauseous scandal after an irreproachable career in the public service! His own wife, the austere, gentle Pomponia, in birth and habit the peeress of any Roman lady, to be soiled by the very suggestion that she had anything to do with licentious alien magic—it was monstrous! No doubt his more steadfast friends gathered round to sympathize, maybe the rough Vespasian among them, and surely the villa gossips discussed such a spicy case. What could Pomponia Graecina have been doing? Ladies of fashion who had toyed with the Jewish cult would make anxious inquiry about their own position, only to be reassured; for Judaism was recognized and approved by the State. It could not have been that, but something sinister, disgraceful—perhaps the pseudo-Jewish sect about which there had been those intriguing stories?

The decree of the Senate had to be obeyed. Presently Pomponia Graecina appeared before her husband and members of his family for questioning. It is reasonable to assume that Aulus Plautius had 'packed' the jury: at all events, they acquitted her of the charge and no further action was taken. Pomponia resumed her sober ways, living to a great age respected by every one, and dying, it is believed, around the year A.D. 90.

Tacitus, who records this episode, gives no detail concerning the accusation. "Foreign superstition" was a phrase used to cover any unauthorized religion. The possibility that Pomponia

Graecina was a Christian was for centuries no more than a likely speculation; but in Victorian times the archaeologist De Rossi, on uncovering a Christian crypt dating from early in the second century, found the inscription "Pomponius Graecinus," thus proving that her family included members of the faith a few years after her death. It need no longer seriously be doubted that she belonged to the community, and that she is the earliest representative of the Roman nobility, so far as knowledge goes, to have accepted the Cross. Thus, within twenty-eight years of his obscure felon's death in far-off Palestine, the Galilean had at least one worshipper who was familiar with the Imperial family in Rome.

Why these proceedings should have been brought against Pomponia Graecina is a mystery. Perhaps spite induced somebody to lay the information—somebody who bore ill-will towards her husband. It was an isolated case. No persecution of the Christian group followed, but the incident must have focused their worried attention, and it may well have had the effect of checking the progress of the new faith among the Jews, who knew to their cost how important it was not to flout the Roman law. Evidence was soon forthcoming that, contrary to experience in some other centres, the Jews in Rome were not easily to be won over, and that the Church recruited its growing strength largely from the Gentiles. Yet it seems to have been in the house of a Jewish couple that its headquarters were established.

Aquila and Priscilla, his wife, were originally from Pontus, in Asia Minor. During the reign of Claudius they had settled in Rome, but were driven out in a persecution of their race. They went to Corinth, where Paul first met them and lodged with them. When the Apostle decided to return to Asia they sailed with him and lived for a spell at Ephesus before going back to Rome, where they appear to have rallied the Christians round them. A degree of holiness and prestige attached to this faithful pair because they were intimates of the renowned Paul, like him being tent-makers, and it is possible they had met Simon Peter himself in the course of their Asian travels. Tent-making was an itinerant craft, probably associated with other skills in the shaping of goatskin and fur; a tent-maker's dwelling in the teeming capital, where city prices prevailed, cannot have been a spacious house. There, however, the nucleus of the Church in Rome was to be found, and those who assembled most likely contributed from their modest purses for its maintenance. It could be that one or two more affluent proselytes, like Pomponia Graecina, were numbered among them.

Nothing is more remarkable than the faith and tenacity with which these first Christian groups held together. Of course, they interchanged many messages, receiving and giving encouragement and advice, and there was a steady coming and going of personalities. But great distances lay between them, communication was slow and unreliable, and, so far as Rome was concerned, no disciple or Apostle burning with the fire of nearness to Jesus had so far visited them. The secret may be found in the conditions of the time. It was one of those periods when, despite frenetic physical activity, the spirit of man was near to death.

Staggering personal wealth moved ruthlessly amid grinding poverty and appalling sickness. The stern morality imposed by the necessities of more primitive existence was no longer required. Luxury had arrived, to be wallowed in by those who could afford it. Bloody circuses pandered to, and ensured the continuance of, the mob's depraved taste. Wit was cynical, learning uncompassionate, vice deliberately cultivated, and cruelty rampant. The mind had outgrown the gods, whose nonsensical mythology was begining to be seen in its right perspective, and the divinity accorded the Emperor was real only because all power was vested in him, and no material conception of godliness could challenge that. Yet man hungered, as he must always hunger, for consolation and assurance to make his condition bearable.

History is like the night sky. The lambent moon and the brilliant stars are picked out, but the vast silent firmament across which they move has no form or vividness. So the enormity of sorrow and the groaning toil that lay behind the figures and events of pagan times go unrecorded and are apt to be unrealized. Gaius Petronius we see; the broken-hearted galley slave, the whipped and tortured 'barbarians' on whose suffering

his capacity to live in abandoned opulence depended—these we
do not see. It is not difficult to grasp what it must have meant to
such as these when the proclamation shone through the darkness that God is love and that, in the person of a provincial
carpenter, his son had died the death of the oppressed to prove
it. All those who laboured and were heavy-laden were freely
called to his tender care.

Not many months after the Pomponia Graecina affair there
arrived at the house where Aquila and Priscilla lived a Greek
woman named Phebe. She had travelled across the narrow sea
from Corinth, and she carried an important letter from Paul. He
had dictated it to Tertius of the Church at Corinth, from whose
members it brought greetings; but it also contained an exciting
promise—Paul intended to come to Rome, though he must first
return with gifts to the mother Church at Jerusalem. (During
this visit to Jerusalem he was rescued by the Romans and
brought before Felix, as already described.)

It is possible to imagine the first reading of the Epistle to the
Romans in the spring of A.D. 58, probably in Aquila's house,
behind closed shutters and barred doors. Candle-light would
flicker on the faces of those who had come to hear. They were
men and women, bond and free, some clad in rough homespun,
some in finer linen, but all passionately attentive as they listened
to the sonorous Greek, read aloud and translated into the Latin
idiom. Paul addressed himself in particular to the backward
Jews at Rome, expounding the catholicity of the faith, but to
Jew and Gentile alike in that room the authoritative words were
laden with consequence. real as life and death. Their eyes must
have shone with anticipation when, towards the end, he told
them his plans:

> Now, having no more place in these parts and having a great
> desire these many years to come unto you; whensoever I take
> my journey into Spain I will come to you; for I trust to see you
> in my journey and to be brought on my way thitherward by you,
> if first I may be somewhat filled with your company. But now I
> go unto Jerusalem to minister unto the saints. For it hath pleased
> them of Macedonia and Achaia to make a certain contribution
> for the poor saints which are at Jerusalem. . . . When therefore
> I have performed this and have sealed to them this fruit, I will

come by you into Spain. And I am sure that when I come unto
you I shall come in the fullness of the blessing of the Gospel of
Christ.

So the Apostle was going to Spain, but would stay a while in
Rome on his way. They must make ready for him in due time,
and some of them must prepare to accompany him towards the
west. The reading voice moved on, and pleasure illumined the
faces of those whom the writer greeted by name, thereby unconsciously recording them for posterity. Two in particular
would be moved, for he acknowledged that they had been
Christians before he himself had met that blinding vision on
the Damascus road more than twenty-five years ago:

> Greet Priscilla and Aquila, my helpers in Christ Jesus . . .
> likewise greet the church that is in their house. Salute my well-
> beloved Epaenetus, who is the firstfruits of Achaia unto Christ.
> Greet Mary, who bestowed much labour on us. Salute Andronicus
> and Junia, my kinsmen, and my fellow-prisoners, who are of
> note among the apostles, who also were in Christ before me.
> Greet Amplias, my beloved in the Lord. Salute Urbane, our
> helper in Christ, and Stachys, my beloved. Salute Apelles
> approved in Christ. Salute them which are of Aristobulus' house-
> hold. Salute Herodion, my kinsman. Greet them that be of the
> household of Narcissus, which are in the Lord. Salute Tryphena
> and Tryphosa, who labour in the Lord. Salute the beloved Persis,
> which laboured much in the Lord. Salute Rufus, chosen in the
> Lord, and his mother and mine. Salute Asyncritus, Phlegon,
> Hermas, Patrobas, Hermes and the brethren which are with
> them. Salute Philologus, and Julia, Nereus and his sister, and
> Olympas, and all the saints which are with them. Salute one
> another with an holy kiss. The churches of Christ salute you. . . .
> The grace of our Lord Jesus Christ be with you all. Amen.

The names in that roll may be taken as including most who
were prominent in the Roman Church at the time. It offers a
tantalizing glimpse into two wealthy estates, those of Aristobulus and Narcissus, whose slaves and freedmen are meant by
the word "household"—not the families, but those who waited
on them. While precise identification cannot be proved, there
is a probability that the men concerned were two known friends
of Claudius Caesar who lived in riches and influence at Rome
and between them might well have measured their households

D

in hundreds. Aristobulus belonged to the Herodian family from
Palestine. His young kinsman and namesake was now married
to the dancing Salome, Philip's widow. Narcissus, until his death
a year or two before this time, had been among Claudius's
fondest intimates. It is likely that, if this was the Narcissus
intended by Paul, his glitteringly endowed family continued in
the style to which they had been accustomed, and that his estate
might yet bear his name.

Thus the Christians in the Imperial capital may be conceived
as being drawn largely from the poorer classes, though a few
richer individuals shared their simple services and helped the
common fund. They were of mixed race—Greeks, Italians,
Asians, and Hebrews. With their co-religionists of Corinth,
Ephesus, Antioch, and Pergamos they maintained an irregular
correspondence—perhaps also with the "poor saints" in Jerusalem itself. They waited not only for the arrival of Paul into
their midst, but also for the early coming of Christ apparelled
in heavenly splendour. They were a people set apart from the
flamboyance in which the life of the city span recklessly.

Yet how many of those thus named by Paul in the Epistle
to the Romans were soon to meet a martyr's death at Nero's
command? Unknowingly he had written their epitaph: "The
churches of Christ salute you."

5

The Honey-haired

SOME two or three years after the crucifixion of Jesus a daughter had been born into a Roman equestrian family. As Poppaea Sabina she was destined to symbolize a type of the scarlet woman in the developing world tragedy whose theme was the conflict of flesh and spirit. Fleshly she was, but a chilling heart lay under her warm breast; an artful and unscrupulous brain functioned at speed behind her lovely brow. Her mother had been a famous beauty who had committed suicide rather than fall a victim to the envious Messalina; Poppaea's physical appearance was even more compulsive, for she concentrated her nimble and experienced mind on its exploitation. By deftly conceding or withholding sexual favours of variegated kind she set out to fulfil a towering ambition.

Moving in the fashionable world of Rome, she quickly seized the opportunity, when it presented itself, of advancing towards the palace. The ardent Otho, like many another man, fell wildly in love with her, and she made no difficulty about leaving her husband to become Otho's wife. It was a considerable step forward. His passion for her became notorious. The rake had been captured by one in whom the inflammatory art of withdrawal and evasion was superbly developed. She knew that nature had endowed her with a maddeningly desirable person, and by the habit of ostentatiously veiling herself, covering her bosom and face, she evinced a strategy that only one utterly confident in her power dared have practised; knowing, too, that its very novelty would have a singular appeal to men of profligate coarseness. Otho, privileged to uncover the riches that were provokingly hidden from other men's eyes, boasted. There never was such perfection as Poppaea's. The transports she stimulated were beyond the comprehension of men accustomed to embracing only ordinary beauties. So, during a fateful conversation, he raved to Nero, inevitably arousing curiosity in that vain mind and desire in its greasy habitation.

The Emperor summoned Poppaea to his presence. He was instantly enslaved. To do him justice, he found she had other attractions about which the clumsier extrovert Otho was indifferent. There was a darting wit beneath the folds of her celebrated honey-coloured hair, and her mouth was merry with raillery. Gaiety she loved—and did not he? But she was also intrigued by the baffling mystery of life and fate—did not such thoughts haunt him too? Her interest in astrology, soothsaying, and Oriental cults was more than a fashionable one. The bent that led her to establish her personal allure by making it mysterious was akin to that which induced her to study horoscopy and magic. Josephus, who met her, defined her as a "religious woman." Political acumen and flattery were no doubt in that assessment; but she was already associated with the Jews, their faith and its ancient rites. She made many friends among them, and is thought by some to have been actually converted. Certainly she was a powerful aide to Jewish causes when, as now happened, she became the Emperor's mistress.

Nero wasted no time. A peremptory instruction sent Otho to an administrative post in far-off Lusitania: his wife was left behind to strew Caesar's pillow with her amber locks.

At this point wise heads like that of Seneca began to realize the futility of trying to check Nero's predilections. What advice and practical help were given to Claudia Acte when the new mistress sailed in can only be presumed; but she managed to elude a rigorous penalty by quietly slipping away to a villa that seems to have been provided for her at Velitrae, and no attempt was made to molest her. From Poppaea's point of view she was contemptible—a plaything that had now been cast aside, that had no significant hold on the Emperor's affections. Yet the gentle Acte remained constant and revealed both her inexperience and womanliness by putting up a shrine to Ceres and beseeching the goddess that in due season Nero would return to her. He never did. He abandoned himself entirely to Poppaea, and she began to mould him to her will by playing on those baser instincts against which he had no strong-minded defence. Under his supervision the games became more ambitious. His love of the fantastic displayed itself, together with pantomimic symbolism. To the mob's delight the Emperor himself began modestly to perform, sometimes representing a god. For one festival the amphitheatre was flooded and a mock battle took place between rival fleets. From the same water Caesar drew up carefully trapped fish on lines of coloured fabric. Bull-fights and encounters between bears and lions were staged. Nero made himself a notable charioteer, driving frenziedly, and was occasionally allowed to lose a race so that reality might be simulated and his magnanimous nature demonstrated by generous gestures and fond smiles. Green being the political colour favourable to the throne, he had green-dyed sand scattered on the circus and dressed himself in green livery for one particular race. He affected various eccentricities in dress, shocking the sturdier Romans by his partiality for soft cloths and effeminate robes from the East. To counteract his short sight he carried a quizzing-glass cut from an emerald. A company of well-drilled young men were present on public occasions to lead the applause and utter such 'spontaneous' cries as were appropriate—"O joy of Rome! Divine father!" and so forth.

But in the secrecy of the domestic apartments, where Poppaea was to be fondled and her intriguing mind revealed its cunning, other ideas were set in motion. Poppaea knew that so long as Nero's mother lived her own path would be set with difficulty and obstruction. She induced her lover first to contemplate and finally to perpetrate Agrippina's murder. An attempt to drown her in a faked accident in the Bay of Naples having failed, other speedy measures had to be adopted, for the victim had been alerted to the plot and might gather supporters to strike back. An instrument was to hand.

The history of the time might have been devised by a master playwright. In detail as in major theme dramatic conflict is vivid. Clashing personalities, contrasting views of light and shade, good and evil, flesh and spirit, treachery and faithfulness, sweep across the stage. Such opposing forces were embodied in the two men who held martial power in Italy. Afranius Burrus, the Praetorian Prefect in charge of the metropolitan soldiery, was a Brutus in his age—"the noblest Roman of them all," brave, tolerant, and enlightened. But in the person of the freedman Anicetus, Prefect of the Fleet, every despicable quality had a harbourage. Only too willing to do the Emperor that kind of favour no decent man may render, he arranged Agrippina's death as she lay abed. O unhappy fate! O malevolent deed! The Emperor's grief was howled from the house-tops lest the people should suspect what everybody else knew—that he had added matricide to his other enterprises. He is reported to have examined his mother's body carefully, praising the perfection of her limbs. But in his heart he experienced a dizzy joy, as if he had been liberated; and the realization that nobody now dare put a brake on his supreme power stimulated increasing madness. He leapt into excesses that hold a fascination for the onlooker because they are refined by an imagination lost to reason.

Men in far-off places felt the impact of his impetuous will in actions that often followed Poppaea's prompting. That Croesus named Pallas, that creature of Claudius's who had been in Agrippina's confidence—he had better make himself scarce! And that brother of his in Judaea—Felix—the Jews were telling strange tales about his mercenary behaviour. Fetch him back, recall him, let him give an account of himself at the Imperial tribunal!

It was the year A.D. 60 when the blow fell on Felix. He was ordered to Rome; his governorship was ended. If he had trembled on hearing Paul's admonition he must have trembled more when Nero's summons came, for his dubious practices, in which blackmail was suspected, had caused much murmuring among the Jews, whose honey-haired friend at Rome now held the Emperor in her arms. The all-powerful must be obeyed, and down the broad front of Caesarea Felix must drive—he and the beautiful Drusilla and their son—escorted for the last time by a clattering cavalcade, past the white amphitheatre and Herod's quadruple gate to the breakwater and the waiting ship.

Although Felix is unlikely to have had any final interview

with Paul, his departure was a matter of moment to the captive Apostle. Paul had now been in Caesarea for nearly two years. He does not seem to have been kept in prison, but it is impossible to say what amount of liberty he was permitted. In any case there was one man living at Caesarea who must have been in constant touch with him to give him help and comfort. This was Philip the Evangelist. (He is not to be confused with the Galilean disciple of the same name who figures in that enchanting pastoral scene which reveals the humour of Jesus—"Behold, an Israelite indeed in whom there is no guile!") Philip was one of seven deacons who had been chosen by the Eleven soon after the Resurrection to help in administering the affairs of the Nazarene community. Stephen, since martyred, had been another.

Philip would have known Christ in the flesh. As a Christian he was, of course, senior to Paul, and may well have been a man in his sixties by this time. He lived with his four daughters, who were devoted to the faith. Paul had lodged at their house on his last journey, as Luke did now, and it is inconceivable that during his stay at Caesarea he did not see a lot of both men. Credulity is not stretched by a picture of the three discussing Paul's plans. That intended visit to Spain, about which he had written to the church at Rome, may well have been talked over. as also the strategy to be adopted when Felix's successor came and in due course called the prisoner for examination.

Festus was the name of the new governor. Soon after his arrival he made a formal visit to Jerusalem, where the Temple priesthood quickly raised the question of the obnoxious Paul, Festus invited them to renew their charge against the Apostle in his presence at Caesarea, and this they did a fortnight later, accusing him of many religious offences. The governor asked Paul whether he would go up to Jerusalem and "there be judged of these things before me?" The answer was prompt. Paul must have thought it over in advance, for while it was irrevocable, it foiled the priesthood. He claimed his right as a Roman citizen with the words: "I appeal unto Caesar." This made certain at least of a visit to Rome, even though it must be in bonds and to await the judgment of the unpredictable Nero.

Nothing more could be done. "Unto Caesar shall you go," was Festus's closure of the case; but the new governor must have found himself personally interested in, and perhaps uneasy about, this remarkable missionary, for a few days later he brought him before Agrippa, the puppet king, and his sister Berenice. They were paying a royal courtesy call at the *praetorium*.

Berenice, older and less spectacular than Drusilla, is yet another of the beautiful women who move like a Chorus to the leading characters in the first-century drama. She has been described as a bigot and a wanton. Professing a deep attachment for the Law, she punctiliously observed its ordinances, but she was capable of treachery. Her wantonness took an unusual form. She had been married and had borne children, but her passion was for her brother, with whom, during phases of her life, she lived incestuously. Misty tradition endows Berenice with glorious golden hair which she is said to have worn loose. Listening to Paul as he debated with her brother that day at Caesarea, she could not have foreseen the ignoble part she was yet to play, within the fold of the Imperial purple, while flame and ruin encompassed her people and their Temple.

Her practised smile must have flashed across the room when Agrippa paid his jesting tribute to Paul's oratory: "Almost thou persuadest *me* to be a Christian!" After all, the only real authority left to Agrippa was the oversight of the Temple, and this remark had its reproachful humour. How incapable the earnest Paul was of taking anything lightly is evident in his answer: "I would to God that not only thou, but also all that hear me this day, were both almost and altogether such as I am, except these bonds."

Human cargo shipped from Judaea to Italy during the summer and early autumn of A.D. 60 was a mixed one. Even before Felix departed a Jewish delegation had gone to complain about him to Nero. The ship in which Paul set forth on his adventurous journey, in charge of the centurion Julius, must have ploughed her way westward only a few weeks later than that bearing Felix and Drusilla, while in his wake followed another Jewish deputation bent on getting Agrippa and the new governor, Festus, into trouble. All roads led to Rome indeed, but owing to shipwreck Paul was not to reach the capital till long after these others had settled their various businesses there.

Those businesses converged not so much on Nero as Poppaea. Ever ready to indict men set in authority over them, the Jews redoubled their efforts when they realized the extent to which they enjoyed Poppaea's goodwill. Just what accusation Felix had to face when he arrived at the Imperial throne cannot be unravelled, nor does he seem to have been punished in any way. The probability is that he was simply dismissed and retired from public life. Both he and Drusilla disappear at this point; only their little son is to be heard of again, piteously. They vanished in the maelstrom of Rome's corrupt society which neither of them held in any disdain.

But the second Jewish delegation, arriving in Rome early in A.D. 61, was to evince striking proof of Poppaea's sympathy. In this case the matter, like that of Pyramus and Thisbe, hinged upon a wall. On top of the Hasmonaean Palace at Jerusalem, where he lived with Berenice, Agrippa had built a penthouse dining-hall. It was high enough for those inside, as they sprawled on their couches, to look into the Temple courts—a profanity the High Priest was not prepared to tolerate. When asked to dismantle this storey Agrippa would not do so, therefore the priests, in turn, put up an intervening wall which blocked his view of the Temple. Angered by such provocation, Agrippa discussed matters with the Roman governor, perhaps because the wall also obstructed the view of Roman sentries at the Tower of Antonia. Festus ordered the priests to pull down the wall. They demanded permission to appeal to Nero, which he gave.

In this controversy there were elements bizarre enough to appeal to the Emperor's love of the unique; but that the judgment was made at Poppaea's behest seems most probable. The Jews were told that they could maintain their wall, and Agrippa and Festus were ordered to withdraw their objections to it. But while eight of the deputation returned joyfully to Jerusalem two of them, Ismael, the High Priest, and Hilkiah, the Keeper of the Treasury, stayed behind in Rome. There may have been some compulsion about this, for in their absence Agrippa appointed a new High Priest, but they were treated as Poppaea's seeming guests, so that she could enjoy the benefit of their instruction and they the further encouragement of her Judaizing tendencies. These bearded dignitaries in their sacerdotal robes added a novel splendour to the voluptuous trappings for which her apartments were now famous. While thus on one hand she dabbled in religion—to what extent and with what sincerity only those scholarly men from Jerusalem would know —on the other she gave full rein to her vanity and love of display, bathing in asses' milk each day to preserve her skin from blemish and ordering that the mules in her stables should be shod with gold lest their feet be polluted by the common pavements.

Meanwhile the Emperor's aberrations took on a darker stain. He was possessed by a desire to overturn, to pervert, to defy the course of nature. His morbid curiosity was insatiate; he cultivated neurotic lusts. He liked to be waited on by notorious prostitutes and to move amid filthy temptations. When he went down the Tiber by boat the town's harlotry was alerted to give ingenious performances on the shore, encouraging him to land and share them. A handsome boy, Sporus, having been castrated, the Emperor tried to have him turned into a woman. "Conscience was a faculty as unknown to Nero as sight to a man born blind."

Towards the strident city sprawled over its seven hills from which this lunatic and his calculating mistress ruled the world there came later that year a straggling party of prisoners. They tramped up the Appian Way, men travel-worn and marked by privation. A few soldiers were in attendance under their centurion Julius. Chains—not heavily weighted—rattled as they paced. Near the centurion strode one to whose infectious courage captives and jailer alike owed their preservation from shipwreck—a wiry, bow-legged man in whom burned a quenchless purpose. On their way from Puteoli a few fellow-Christians had been allowed to join them and share the precious privilege of his company. Perhaps among them was the constant Aquila.

So Paul's eyes at last rested on the Imperial capital. As they did so his great heart must have swollen, remembering that dream at Jerusalem two years ago when a beloved voice had said: "Be of good cheer, Paul; for as thou hast testified of me in Jerusalem so must thou bear witness also at Rome."

6

The Year of Murder

PAUL'S situation was that of a man on remand, waiting for his appeal to be heard. He had arrived in Rome at a time when there was no persecution of Christians: indeed, although the authorities must have heard of them, they could only have been regarded as a non-conforming section of the Jewish population with whom the Rabbis would know how to deal sooner or later. It was presently to be realized that these Christians—whose growth was very rapid after Paul's arrival—were highly objectionable, not on account of their religious ideas, but because they behaved in a manner politically suspicious and socially repugnant. The great stable pillar of the State was the Law of Associations introduced by the Emperor Augustus. It prohibited all societies which failed to register and thus seek permission to hold meetings. Christians never asked for authorization; they met secretly, ate a ceremonial meal behind closed doors, kept away from the ordinary life of the people, and were notably missing from Roman festivals. These, and not their devotion to a criminal who had been put to death in Judaea thirty years before, were the reasons why the Roman power came to hold them in abhorrence. They were felt to be plotting against national institutions, like so many active Communist cells. Moreover, they consisted very largely of the dispossessed, the enslaved, the scum from beside the Tiber.

But from A.D. 61 to 63, the period of St Paul's detention in Rome, there was no perceptible movement against the Christians. Everything was otherwise. The sect prospered astonishingly, winning converts and openly engaging in evangelistic work. On arrival at Rome Paul automatically came into the custody of the Praetorian Prefect, the temperate Burrus. It is

very doubtful if they ever met. The Apostle would be handed
over to some subordinate of the Minister—the captain of the
guard in the first instance. The circumstances of his life were
not irksome; he seems to have been given considerable liberty.
Whether the lodgings he rented were attached to the *praetorium*
itself—the great military headquarters with barracks and
stables—or whether they were actually in the outer precincts of
the palace cannot be said. It is one of the details about which
historians argue and is incapable of resolution. A soldier lived
with him, so that he was kept under surveillance, and when he
moved out he would be chained to the man: chained prisoners
were probably so commonplace in Rome as not to merit a second
glance from passers-by.

Following his usual practice, Paul endeavoured to win over
the Jewish population, inviting leaders of the synagogues to
hear him. But, as hitherto, the Jews of Rome generally were not
to be persuaded. Thereupon he concentrated on the Gentiles.
His own words, written in his letter to the Philippians in A.D. 62,
are plain and revealing: "But I would you should understand,
brethren, that the things which happened unto me have fallen
out rather unto the furtherance of the Gospel; so that my bonds
in Christ are manifest in all the palace and in all other places;
and many of the brethren in the Lord, waxing confident by my
bonds, are much more bold to speak the Word without fear."
The epistle ends: "The brethren which are with me greet you.
All the saints salute you, chiefly they that are of Caesar's household."

Filling in the details calls for no difficult exercise. Preaching,
baptizing, contending, the Apostle moved amid the soldiers,
slaves, and busy bureaucratic freedmen in his immediate neighbourhood. Among the palace staff—which would embrace all
such—a Christian party had been definitely established.
Although it was 'below stairs,' it is hard to believe that it could
have existed for many months without more substantial persons
becoming acquainted with it. Again one wonders what tidings
reached Claudia Acte at Velitrae from those about the palace
who had known her and probably pitied her condition.

When Paul wrote of "the brethren which are with me" he

would have particularly in mind Mark, who after a dispute during their Asian mission many years earlier, had become reconciled to him in Rome; Luke, a physician and native of Antioch, his travelling companion and author of the Acts of the Apostles; Aristarchus, a fellow-prisoner from Palestine; Timothy, the Apostle's amanuensis and young disciple; Silvanus; and one Demas, who was in harder days to forsake him. They were a powerful phalanx of the faith, and two of them were to compile the Gospels that bear their names. During his two years in Rome Paul wrote also his letters to Ephesus and Colossae. His lodging was the centre of ceaseless endeavour, and literally hundreds must have waited upon him. The conclusion is that not only was he treated with tolerance, but the immediate authorities must have shown more than a little sympathy towards him. Obviously a man so exceptional, under an enthusiasm so superior, would command the respectful attention of the soldiery around him—a soldiery that took its code of conduct from its venerated Prefect, Burrus.

But for Burrus death was at hand. The year A.D. 62 is laden with pitiless crime and marks the beginning of Nero's insensate phase. While Paul spent his days and nights in prayer and preaching, a short distance away in the exalted chambers of the palace there was hatched an infamous conspiracy. Its instigation must lie to the charge of Poppaea, though at every stage Nero provided the necessary decree.

Poppaea could not marry the Emperor because Octavia, his wife, still lived—and Poppaea was pregnant. Her child must be born legally into the purple. Nero repeatedly raised the question of a divorce with his advisers, but on this Burrus was adamant. "If you want to divorce her," he said, "you must give her back her dowry." By this he meant the Empire itself, for she was Claudius's daughter. To Nero's persistence Burrus replied with words that betray a menacing manner: "When I say something once don't pester me to say it again!" Nobody else had the guts to use speech like that to the Emperor; but it was probably the astute Poppaea, rather than Nero, who realized its implications. Burrus was a man of whom such a woman as Poppaea would stand in some awe and not a little fear. That he did not intend her to be Empress she realized, but, further than this, instinct would tell her that he was the one man in Rome who might decide at any moment to rid the world both of her paramour and herself. It is a fair speculation that, had Burrus lived, he would within months have drawn his sword against Nero, and that the enormities which blackened the following years would not have taken place. Yet without the mass martyrdom of A.D. 64, would Christianity have received its conquering impetus?

Burrus did not live. He was poisoned. In a quaint wish to modify posterity's judgment of Nero some latter-day historians have clung to the official tale that he died of a throat affliction. Suetonius knew better. His death occurred in a very timely hour from Poppaea's point of view. The loathsome Tigellinus was appointed one of two Praetorian Prefects, and the task of getting rid of poor Octavia was put in hand. But before this could be done Seneca decided that it was time to save his own skin—at any rate, for the present. Burrus, his friend, had paid the price of being honest in the State's service. Seneca withdrew from public life, applying himself entirely to his pen. Some of his Stoic philosophy embodies arguments in harmony with Christian doctrine, and has led to the suggestion that he had dealings with Paul. While it is obviously not impossible, there is no reliable evidence for this. Pauline Christianity, intent on welding the truth of the Jewish Messiah into Graeco-Latin thought, caught reflexes of a climate to which Seneca also was responsive.

Poppaea endeavoured to prove that Octavia had committed adultery with an Egyptian flute-player, but she failed to secure false witnesses. Instead, Nero divorced his wife on the ground that she was sterile. Within a fortnight Poppaea became the Empress; but the unpredictable mob took the part of Octavia, and when a rumour seized them that the Emperor, having relented, was about to recall his first wife their joy knew no bounds. Crowds milled through the streets, overthrowing Poppaea's statues and replacing them with Octavia's, which they garlanded. Swords and staves were used by the soldiers before order was restored. In the calm that followed Poppaea sank, a suppliant, at Nero's feet. Did he not realize that, in Octavia backed by the mob, he had now a rival for the throne itself?

He did. He knew these haughty Claudians. He had been a fool to divorce her on such an unconvincing charge: the people probably knew he had given her little opportunity to disprove her sterility. But how find another accusation? How? A man, of course, was needed who would make appropriate confession for appropriate reward. A man? Why, who more serviceable, more eager to be of service, than Anicetus, Prefect of the Fleet? Had he not dealt with the awkward problem of Agrippina when nobody else would?

Anicetus was only too delighted once more to succour his Emperor. The nauseating creature declared before a convention of Ministers that Octavia had frequently committed adultery with him. Having provided this necessary 'evidence,' he was permitted to retire from the naval service, and he lived comfortably in Sardinia for the rest of his peaceful and contented life. But Octavia, adjudged guilty of treason, adultery, and abortion, was banished to the island of Pandateria, near the Bay of Naples.

Presumably all this befouling business had to be gone through for the sake of protocol, for the conspirators had made up their minds how it was going to end. Octavia was placed under military supervision in Pandateria, and within a week or two the soldiers got their expected order. On June 9 they carried it out; they killed her. She was only twenty-two. She had lived a blameless life. She pleaded with the swordsman: "I am no longer Nero's wife; I cannot do him any harm now." They cut off her head, and presently, in the palace, it was rolled out of its bloody cloth and displayed at the feet of Poppaea. The obsequious Senate led the nation in thanksgiving to the gods that the girl had been so safely disposed of. Yet in the very midst of this Roman cesspool that selfsame year Paul wrote: "Finally, brethren, whatsoever things are true, whatsoever things are honest, whatsoever things are just, whatsoever things are pure, whatsoever things are lovely, whatsoever things are of good report—if there be any virtue and if there be any praise, think on these things." Such was the contrast, such the going down and rising of the sun, at Rome in A.D. 62.

It is habitual to depict the earliest Christian groups as living so much to themselves and being so absorbed in their meditations that they ignored the life around them. This is sentimental illusion. The influence of contemporary events is to be found throughout their writings, and who is to say that the villainous sequence ending in poor Octavia's death played no part in Paul's exhortation to hold fast to the things that are more excellent? Surely, his dwelling close to the Praetorian barracks and the armoury inspired his figurative language in the letter to the Ephesians—about the breastplate of righteousness, the helmet of salvation, and the sword of the spirit? One can imagine him watching soldiers putting on their gear.

Another famous epistle had now made its appearance among the Jewish adherents of Christianity. It came from the East. In spite of repeated subjection to critical analysis it has been found impossible to destroy the tradition that attributes it to the stepbrother of Jesus. The Epistle of James is the work of a Christian Pharisee: it is intensely Hebrew in its maintenance of the Law, yet the Greek in which it is written has a scholarly grace. Here, again, if it is accepted that the author was James, the writer is aware of surrounding conditions:

> From whence come wars and fightings among you? . . . Ye lust and have not; ye kill and desire to have, and cannot obtain. . . . Go to now, ye rich men, weep and howl for your miseries that shall come upon you. Your riches are corrupted and your garments are motheaten. Your gold and silver is cankered.

These phrases reflect the ominous decay that had set in throughout Judaea, a decay typical of all pre-revolutionary periods. Lawlessness was rampant in the streets and cynical corruption festered in high places. Rebellious bands followed a diversity of leaders. Jerusalem was terrorized by a campaign of indiscriminate murder, carried out by *sicarii*, or dagger-men. They killed in broad daylight; none knew when or whom they would strike. They carried knives under their cloaks, mingled with the crowds, and when they had stabbed their victim joined vehemently in the indignation of passers-by. It is easy to realize how demoralizing such a campaign could quickly become. Yet this was only a part of the public distress. Factions employed

E

by the High Priest fought with supporters of the people. All the underworld was encouraged to violence. The roads were infested with robbers and the hills sheltered ruthless banditti.

The priestly caste and the Sadducees—"ye rich men," as James called them—had grown fat on the degraded exercise of their privileges. They practised every available form of extortion and blackmail, even prostituting Temple customs. The Levites wore gloves rather than that their hands should be bloodstained when they handled the sacrifices. Israel was worshipping the golden calf again, and those who tried to keep faith with Moses were appalled and helpless. By intermittent assault the Roman power seemed to make matters worse, and when Festus died suddenly at the beginning of A.D. 62 and the province was left without a governor confusion was intensified and opportunities for malevolence were widened.

Amid this desperate anarchy the Jewish Christians, "the poor saints in Jerusalem," remained calm and steadfast. It is possible that, forming the only apparent rallying-point for all who clung to common morality, they were supported by non-Christian Pharisees in their stern opposition to the faithless priesthood. At their head, venerated by every good element in the city, was James, "the Lord's brother."

James was now an old man. His life for years had been a model of devoted piety in the eyes of all beholders. He was known as "the Just One." His austerity was described by Hegesippus a generation later:

> To him alone it was permitted to enter the holy place; for he wore nothing woollen, but linen garments. And alone he entered into the sanctuary and was found on his knees asking forgiveness on behalf of the people, so that his knees became hard like a camel's, for he was continually bending the knee in worship to God and asking forgiveness for the people. On account of his exceeding great justice he was called "the Just" and "Oblias," which is in Greek "bulwark of the people."

For this rock-like and beloved figure the Temple aristocracy harboured an envious hatred. The High Priest at this time was an arrogant Sadducee named Ananus, whose jealousy of the Christians impelled him to take precipitate action when Festus died. What he and his heirarchy dared not have done under the eyes of a Roman governor they did in the interval before Festus's successor arrived. James was hauled before them and, in some form or other, was asked to repudiate Christ. When he refused he was cast headlong down the Temple steeps—possibly into the stoning-pit outside the wall, for Josephus says he was stoned. The fall did not kill the old man, according to Hegesippus, whereupon a bystander beat him to death with a fuller's staff.

So died James the Just—only a few hundred yards away from the place where his stepbrother, Jesus, had been crucified thirty-three years earlier—carrying with him recollections of a boyhood in Nazareth.

An angry cry ran through Jerusalem at this outrage, and a number of indignant citizens (who do not appear to have been predominantly Christian) hastened southward to meet the governor-designate, Albinus, then making his way towards Judaea from Egypt. Albinus too was angry. He sent a scorching rebuke to the High Priest for having dared to put anybody to death—and others beside James perished at Ananus's hands—and insisted on Agrippa's dismissing him. These consequences illustrate at once Rome's religious tolerance at that time and the popular support enjoyed by James the Just.

Bereft of the great man who had been their mainstay and inspiration for some twenty years, the Christians in Jerusalem gathered to choose a new leader. They regarded themselves as the fount of the faith, the pure Word spoken by the Galilean Messiah who had observed the Mosaic Law and preached in the Temple courts. In their eyes, as the Gentile churches of Asia and Europe moved away from Judaism, so they moved away from their founder, Jesus the Nazarene. Christianity was a Jewish development, cradled in Israel, native to the circumcision. Eusebius affirms that among those who met in the Jerusalem conference, which must have taken place in the summer of A.D. 62, were some of the Apostles "together with our Lord's relatives after the flesh, for the more part of them were still alive." Their resolve to hold fast to the Galilean family was made plain by their decision. They chose as their leader Simeon, the son of Cleophas, and therefore in this sense a cousin of Jesus Christ. His mother, Mary Cleophas, had been among those women who stood by the cross.

Though the office of bishop had not been formulated at so early a date, Simeon is listed as the second Bishop of Jerusalem, James having been the first. As Jesus nominally was himself, so both these men were of the line of David.

7

The Two Apostles

SOMEWHERE Sir Winston Churchill has written: "The historian of ill-recorded times has none the less to tell his tale." It is a remark that springs to mind when endeavouring to solve the tantalizing mystery embedded in the five years, A.D. 63 to 68—how did the great Apostles Peter and Paul meet their deaths? There is not a wisp of direct evidence. That they died during the reign of Nero seems beyond doubt, and the weight of early tradition that they were martyred in Rome is so mountainous that no critic has seriously questioned its accuracy. On the other hand, the once generally held assumption that they perished during the Neronian massacre in A.D. 64 is no longer, and for good reasons, willingly conceded.

Had Peter been a victim in A.D. 64 it is well-nigh impossible that he could have been responsible for the First Epistle that bears his name. This letter is addressed to the faithful in the far Asian provinces—Galatia, Cappadocia, Pontus, Bithynia. It is a message of encouragement to people about to come under the sufferings of persecution:

> Beloved, think it not strange concerning the fiery trial which is to try you, as though some strange thing happened unto you; but rejoice in as much as ye are partakers of Christ's suffering. . . . But let none of you suffer as a murderer, or as a thief, or as an evildoer, or as a busybody in other men's matters. Yet if any man suffer as a Christian, let him not be ashamed, but let him glorify God on this behalf. . . . Your adversary the devil, as a roaring lion, walketh about, seeking whom he may devour: whom resist stedfast in the faith, knowing that the same afflictions are accomplished in your brethren that are in the world. But the God of all grace, who hath called us unto his eternal glory by Christ Jesus, after that ye have suffered a while, make you perfect, stablish, strengthen, settle you.

There was no persecution of Christians in any organized sense whatever, or in any part of the Empire, before A.D. 64. It was Nero in that year who began the "fiery trail" which afterwards spread across Asia and Gaul. Could words like these have been penned before then?

Modern critics deny that the epistle was written by Peter or that he had anything to do with it: they argue that it refers to some second great persecution said to have taken place under the Emperor Domitian after A.D. 90. But this is to accept the now discredited view that the Christians suffered only in certain well-defined major oppressions, whereas it is clear that from 64 onward, once the signal had been given in Rome, martyrdom was imposed in sporadic outbreaks in many parts of the Empire—particularly in the East. Other argument against the authorship of Peter is that commonly held against so much of the New Testament—the Greek is too good, the phraseology too eloquent, "for a Galilean fisherman." Only by the charitable concession that scholars are notoriously not worldly-wise can this kind of reasoning be allowed. Peter and Paul were both men of action. They were not literary artists. It is plain for all to see that they employed secretaries who would be—at least in respect of the old fisherman—more erudite. These were younger men eager to put the thoughts of their revered elders into effective and persuasive Greek. So far as Paul is concerned, of course, direct authorship is frequently evident; moreover, the impassioned rhetoric he sometimes dictated broke down any attempt at secretarial 'improvement.' But the Galileans must have left a great deal to their scribes.

Even so—as in the case of other epistles and Gospels—the personality of the real author shines through; and there is not a point, reflection, or exhortation in Peter I that could not have come from the direct-minded fisherman. On the contrary, there is touching evidence that his Master's words were well-remembered. "Feed my sheep" was Jesus's last command to Peter. "Feed the flock of God that is among you" was Peter's command to those addressed in this epistle. Criticism must continually challenge documents so important as these, but due regard should always be given to the fact that they were admitted to the canon—that is, accepted as genuine—only after scrupulous testing and debate by the primitive Church. In one or two instances where even canonical books are subject to some doubt the doubts were early expressed and put on record for the guidance of later generations. Peter I does not come in this category. Eusebius comments: "Of Peter one epistle, his former as it is called, is acknowledged; and of this the elders of olden times have made frequent use, as a work beyond dispute, in their own treatises."

Accepting this document, then, as having been composed by direction of Simon Peter the disciple, acknowledging that it could not have been written earlier than the late summer of A.D. 64, and that Peter died before the end of Nero's reign in June A.D. 68, what probabilities emerge?

The epistle was written from Rome: this is manifest in the concluding passage, where the author says: "The church that is at Babylon . . . saluteth you." Rome, the "great harlot," was often disguised as "Babylon" in communications between Christians under persecution. But the letter was carried by Silvanus, and it included greetings from Mark—two of those who, as we have seen, were working with Paul at Rome in A.D. 62. They were now working with Peter. Yet in the epistles Paul wrote from Rome no reference is made to Peter's being there; similarly, Peter makes no mention of Paul.

The last recorded meeting between these two—indeed, the last authentic statement of Peter's whereabouts—had been at Antioch nearly twenty years earlier. On that occasion they had quarrelled over the extent to which there should be social intimacy between Jews and Gentiles. The quarrel illustrates their differing characteristics. The humourless Paul was versed in dialectic, fanatically earnest, consumed by an overmastering purpose that never seems to have relaxed for an instant and never left him in the slightest doubt about what to do in any set of circumstances. He must have found it difficult at times to suffer the blundering ways of Peter, whose human fallibility (which makes him the more appealing figure to ordinary mortals) seemed to Paul an indictable fault. Peter's generous impulse, and his profound instinct for knowing the will of

THE EASTERN EMPIRE: SITES

EARLIEST CHRISTIAN ACTIVITY

Christ, had made him the first disciple to welcome Gentiles into the fold. Subsequently, at Antioch, he had been rebuked by emissaries from James at Jerusalem for going a little too far by actually eating with Gentiles. That was offensive to Pharisaic rules. Thereupon Peter had withdrawn himself from close association with the uncircumcised: he checked his better nature in order to avoid trouble with the Rabbis. Poor fellow! When Paul, "the Apostle of the Gentiles," presently arrived in Antioch he denounced Peter for being so narrow, and he pulled no punches. "I withstood him to the face," he wrote later.

Was this clash so long ago, were these differences in temperament, sufficient to account for the failure of either Apostle to mention the other, assuming they were both in Rome at the same time? The thought is not seriously to be entertained. For thirty years they had shared an abiding devotion to a supreme cause. They were, both in themselves and in their application to their Saviour's business, men who would rise superior to any such secondary considerations. The conclusion must be that they were *not* in Rome together. This view contradicts a tradition that Peter lived many years in the city, but it accords with certain pointers concerning Paul.

The belief that Paul left Rome at that time rests mainly on three considerations. First, that the Acts of the Apostles states that he spent two years there, implying an end to the stay; second, that the Pastoral Epistles (those to Timothy and Titus), if written by him, involve another journey to the East after his detention in Rome; third, that Clement, in his letter to the Corinthians, written about A.D. 95, strongly suggests that Paul actually completed his avowed intention of going to Spain before he was martyred. These matters will be considered in more detail as they arise in the sequence of this narrative. For the moment it will suffice to present the hypothesis that Paul's appeal was heard by Nero (or his Imperial judges) in A.D. 63, that it was upheld, that he was set free, and that he then left Italy. Of those known to have been attendant on him in Rome he took with him Luke, Timothy, and Demas. Mark and Silvanus remained behind, and when, some time later, Peter arrived they joined him as stated in the context when he wrote his First Epistle.

Whether Peter reached Rome before A.D. 64 and somehow survived the great persecution, or whether he got there soon afterwards to find the Christian remnant scattered, bereaved, and in hiding, can only be conjectured. It is even conceivable that, having received news of their suffering, he followed a typical impulse and hastened to Rome in order to succour, rally, and inspire them.

8

The Nineteenth of July

DURING a great part of the day Nero lay on his couch, compresses round his neck, physicians and singers in attendance. He was not ill; he was nursing his vocal chords, having convinced himself—if none other—that nature had given him a voice of mellifluous beauty. In fact, it was not inharmonious as voices go, but it was small and throaty. Resting it, even from speech, was his particular care; although, by way of contrast, he sometimes depressed his boon companions, like Petronius and Tigellinus, by reciting long and boring odes of his own composition. He would listen for hours to experts, such as Terpnus the musician, who expounded to him everything they knew about their art. Raw leeks, because they soothed and stimulated the larynx, were served to him regularly—a practice that could hardly have pleased the fastidious Poppaea, whose very name was destined to be given to the richest unguents and most elusive perfumes.

The Emperor was now devoted to the arts. He believed he was a poet, a singer, and a fine judge of sculpture. (In fairness to him the Apollo Belvedere is said to have been found beneath one of his houses.) But was Roman taste exquisite enough? Could Rome—rough, militaristic Rome—appreciate its master's talents? Was not his soul Greek and his sense of form Athenian? He longed to go to Greece, to take part in the lyrical competitions; but he compromised by giving his first public performance at a concert in Naples early in A.D. 64. Soon after he left the theatre an earthquake demolished it, and this he considered a divine encouragement. It was as if the gods ordained that, having once been honoured by his voice, the building could have no further useful purpose to fulfil. He dashed off a poem thanking the gods for their favour. Then he thought more about

Greece, changed his mind, and decided to go to Egypt instead. But at the last moment, when about to embark for Alexandria, fear seized him because the omens seemed to be unpropitious. He issued a proclamation saying that he could not bear to see the sorrow on the faces of the people as they contemplated his departure, and had, therefore, resolved to stay with them in Rome.

As relaxation from the exacting demands of art, Nero allowed himself grosser and more luxuriant entertainment. His feasts grew longer—from midday to dawn—and were marked by every possible extravagance and the most ingenious experiments in debauchery. For himself there was the matchless Poppaea to adore—alas, that her girl-child had not lived!—and the constant Sporus was always at hand if he felt disposed towards pederasty. The plebs loved him. What more, other than the plaudits of Greece, which would presently be his, could he wish for? Under his leek-tanged breath his fat body heaved with contentment, sensible of its divine destiny. It was a satisfactory panorama on which he peered through the emerald, his puffy lips blandly smiling. Nero Claudius Caesar Augustus Germanicus had reached the zenith of his life. He was twenty-seven.

When summer temperatures climbed that year he moved the Court from Rome to Antium, his birthplace, a seaside town some thirty-five miles from the capital. Antium is now Anzio, the landing-point made immortal by British and American valour when Italy was rescued from another dictator. Here the Emperor practised his declamation and singing on the unhappy members of a house-party, while the hot nights were murmurous with sleepless life under a velvet sky. In Rome itself July brought its customary stifling conditions, enervating and fever-laden. The well-to-do had gone to their country villas; the poor sweated it out in their tenements and alleys. And suddenly a hotter blast than that of sun or climate swept over them murderously.

It was the night of July 19, A.D. 64. Horrified cries rose from the mass of rickety shops clustered about the end of the Great Circus under the Palatine Hill. They were drowned immediately by the impetuous roar of flame—enormous flame—which, beginning nobody knew how, poured mercilessly forward like a consuming tide, whipped by a strong southerly wind. It ate up shops, storehouses, and stables at an incredible speed. Reaching the long open space of the circus itself, it sprang onward as through a mighty corridor, reinforcing its strength from the thousands of wooden seats stretched along the tiers. Before the night was over the densely populated valley under the Palatine was flooded with writhing flame. Houses and manufacturies collapsed, blocking the thoroughfares. The innumerable narrow ways in the lower quarters were like so many tubes into which the blistering heat was sucked, so that flame leapt spontaneously in fifty places at once wherever there was summer-dry timber to be gripped. The elementary equipment of Rome's fire-brigade was utterly helpless before this holocaust.

Every man, woman, and child in threatened areas of the city sought to escape when the magnitude of the disaster and its more terrifying potential burst upon them. Up the hillsides the conquering flames now mounted, wiping out famous temples and elaborate villas. Well-tended gardens died under the awful breath, trees and shrubs vanishing amid a whirl of reddled smoke. Down below, through district after district, the fury raced, tearing to pieces the very shape of the city. High wind scattered deluges of blazing ash far and wide, igniting further areas. How many died in that first assault will never be known. Through the staircases and corridors of the gaunt tenements where tens of thousands had their miserable homes flame and smoke together poured at killing speed.

Panic seized the hapless people. As they leapt from balustrades or raced into the streets they found their ways of escape barred by ever-new walls of fire or by incandescent mounds of rubble. Roads that were not immediately menaced by flame saw stampeding humans choking by their number the route to safety. The old and infirm were lost; children parted from their parents ran piteously to their own destruction. Baggage wagons, bringing in the city's supplies, must vastly have multiplied obstructions in the streets. Their maddened horses and oxen ploughed amid the battling crowds of human beings. Bridges, statues, colonnades crashed down, adding to the death-roll. Nobody attempted to organize resistance to the fire. Communication was impossible: it was each for himself.

Later dawns, when they came, found Rome obliterated under a huge canopy of smoke while the fire ate its way remorselessly in every direction. Refugees streamed outward clothed in the cries of mourning and pain. Chaos prevailed. Many sought refuge in the tombs and catacombs. The living were numbed by the horror they had passed through: nearly all must have been seared by some sort of personal loss.

For nine days the fire continued. Only four of the city's fourteen administrative regions escaped damage. After the first appalling night and day strenuous efforts were made to contain it. Areas were deliberately devastated so that the flames might be deprived of fuel. When the news reached Antium the Emperor exerted himself at once, ordering relief stores to be hurried forward. He hastened to Rome and helped to direct those who tried to prevent the Imperial palace from being engulfed. They failed, and Nero saw his own residence disappear before his eyes. Nevertheless, he opened his gardens about the Esquiline and every available public building to house the homeless and injured, and he ordered shelters to be set up in the Field of Mars. Bare justice requires such facts to be considered in relation to the stories that began to develop when at last the fire stopped and bewildered men asked the inevitable questions: How did it happen? How can it be accounted for?

From these questions two themes of rumour emerged: that there had been deliberate opposition to fire-fighting by officialdom, and that the Emperor himself had been well-pleased to see the city laid in ashes. It was said that when the conflagration was at its height those who tried to stem the flames were molested by men who compelled them to stop, and even flung burning brands about, spreading the fire. Some said these men were soldiers in disguise, acting under authority. Others declared that Nero had been seen high on a tower on the Esquiline, delirious with joy, harping a Trojan song as he watched the devastation all around. Was he not a wild-eyed poet? Would it not be typical of him to want to replace the old city with some wonderful new imitation of Athens? Had he deliberately set

Rome on fire in order to satisfy his vanity and his dramatic sense? What did it matter to him that the poor suffered grievously?

Whether there was any basis for these reports none can say. Nero's defenders point out that he was at Antium when the outbreak started; his accusers reply that a guilty man would arrange precisely such an absence. But all Rome became murmurous with accusation. Embittered groups gathered amid the ruin of their homes, protesting. Ominous forbodings clouded Authority's brow as echoes of wrath and lamentation rolled round the seven hills. Fear went to bed with the Emperor and chilled him on waking. He emptied his treasury in order to speed the rebuilding of the city. Though it was observed that his biggest undertaking was a new palace—the Golden House of which he had long dreamed, with its parks, lakes, and gardens—he did, in fact, concentrate on rehousing the people; and it was a finer Rome from every point of view that began to rise out of the rubble. Yet all this feverish activity did little to arrest the discontent, the latent revolution.

Anxious councils were held, for the throne was certainly not secure. No wise Seneca, no restraining Burrus, was available now; but Poppaea must have given her advice. Among those most persuasive in her retinue were her Jewish friends. The voice of Jerusalem's Temple would gladly whisper in her pretty ear that the fanatical sect of "Chrestus" was imbued with hatred for the world and preached a fiery dissolution. Aye! the skulking Christians—what of them? Nero jumped at the scapegoat thus offered, but it would appear that rumour was carefully fostered before he came into the open. Down the byways ran malevolent gossip. Was it not a fact that some of those insensate beasts who had flung blazing torches to spread the flames were Christians? Had it not been said repeatedly that these secretive corrupters loved to foretell the end of the world? Were they not bent on stamping out civilization under the prompting of their occult superstition?

Within five weeks of the fire a number of Christians were indicted as incendiaries. Under examination they are said to have accused fellow-Christians, a charge that may well have arisen from their use of prophetic language and from a ready acquiescence in cunningly contrived references to their inflammatory phrases. Some, of course, may have broken down under torture; some turned apostate. At all events a great corralling of the sect took place in which the mob must have joined eagerly. Its blood was up now, and it believed that the abhorrent followers of this Oriental cult were responsible for the disaster. It is not known how many came before Nero and his assessors, but the detailed charges of incendiarism seem to have broken down for lack of real evidence. Nevertheless, as the sect's character became more plain its—to Roman eyes—odious nature emerged, and Christians were denounced as enemies of the human race. They were evildoers, plotters of destruction, haters of all that Rome had created through emancipating centuries. They were seditious, abjurers of the gods, contrivers of malignant mischief, devotees of bestial practices.

No formal law was framed to deal with this situation. Christians were condemned as Christians. They had simply to acknowledge the name to merit death, for the name was held to be infamous. In hunting them down the Roman mob conceived that it was hunting the incendiaries, and Nero won praise for his shrewdness in detecting the criminals. From his standpoint, the more relentlessly the pursuit continued and the more men reviled the Christians, the better it was. Nobody any longer suggested that he had been in any way to blame. Now arose for the first time the cry, "The Christians to the lions!" and Nero made sure that their sufferings should be deep, comprehensive, and exciting—a new game to appease the mob.

The community must have become a substantial one by this time, for although no hint is given by the Roman historian about the number killed, the inference is inescapable that it was large. The persecution of A.D. 64 was an outstanding event in contemporary Roman affairs, second only to the fire itself. Many hundreds, possibly thousands, passed through dire agony to martyrdom. The condemned included men and women, the old, the vigorous, and the young. Some may have broken down, doubtless some relented and sought mercy—though there is no evidence that mercy was ever conceded—but subsequent re-

F

action by the Roman population itself is the clearest evidence that the great majority presented a spectacle of dauntless valour and unfaltering faith.

All who wished to see Rome's enemies meet an appropriate doom were bidden to the amphitheatre. Here there was a rare feast for sadistic eyes. In groups, or singly, Christians were led into the arena to suffer whatever had been prepared for them. Some were devoured by beasts. The lions had their share. Women, in imitation of Dirce, were fastened to the horns of wild bulls; the enraged animals tore and beat them to pieces. A bull that took a long time to finish the task assigned to it roused the mob to mockery; its victim's last memory of earth was the laughter of ridicule. Some of the condemned ones played the parts of those who were to die in scenes from the Greek legends. They underwent all the torments prescribed by the story.

These horrible events appear to have continued for as long as blood-lust could be extended. Novel deaths for selected Christians would 'top the bill' on many a day's performance at the amphitheatre. One favourite device was to cover the victim with animal's skin and have him hunted by a pack of savage hounds. But the appalling climax was staged in Nero's gardens. One night these were open to all comers who wished to enjoy a ravishing spectacle prepared by the Emperor. As they poured into the gates from the city stews the mob found that all along the racecourse avenue crosses and stakes had been erected. To these were bound Christians, men and women, clad each in a garment saturated with oil. At a given signal their "tunics of pain" were lighted; and straightway the Emperor himself, driving a chariot, galloped forward. As the human torches flamed skyward he drove his team among them.

Despite all that has been written commending some of his clear-sighted judgments and kindlier actions, the empurpled wretch obviously floated on seas of delusional insanity. It is a falsely based argument that Nero merely reflected the cruel licence of his age. His fate and the opprobrium he drew from his contemporaries disprove it. There is an account of how, on one occasion, when condemned victims had been tied to stakes he clad himself in the skin of a wild beast and savaged them obscenely. The tongue of slander is hardly ingenious enough to invent such a grotesque scene, or to imagine that other monstrous episode when he went through a marriage ceremony with his creature Sporus. The man was mad. But it is hard to wring pity for him; only Claudia Acte had that to give.

So terrible, so protracted, was the Christian ordeal that even the Roman stomach recoiled and at last fell sick. Mingled with satiety was an unusual compassion. The Emperor was going too far, these people died bravely; let it rest. A dying Christian was no longer an object for scorn, but of pity. In a profoundly suggestive passage Renan has pointed out that the mysterious appeal of physical purity was probably sensed by the Roman crowd for the first time when Christian women and girls were exposed, naked but for a cincture, to the gaze of thousands. Modesty unveiled took on a serene and sacrificial aspect never seen before in their experience. One wonders how many of the poor saints "that are of Caesar's household" escaped the palace security check.

When autumn came the mass murder was over; the charnel houses were glutted. Intermittent persecutions flared up in other parts of the Empire as Rome's example was reported abroad. For, in spite of the armistice that now prevailed in the capital itself, a war had been declared by the Empire on the Cross that was to endure for centuries; sometimes to break out in violent and widespread combat, sometimes to be low-muttering in guerrilla strife. The nature of its end was inevitable from that of its beginning. Had the Christians in A.D. 64 failed to meet the initial onslaught so bravely, setting a standard by which their successors gloried in measuring themselves, it is doubtful how the issue might have gone. But they emulated their Saviour's conduct at Calvary, and against that the Roman power could not prevail.

After the last victim had died and a combination of repletion and boredom had turned the Emperor's attention to fresh fields, the Christian survivors gathered themselves somehow together to count the loss and heal the wounds. They eked out a fugitive existence in cave and catacomb, but they must have maintained a coherent organization otherwise they could never so speedily have become once more an influence in the capital. When one considers the ruthless massacre that had taken place and the awful threat that overhung the living remnant, their will to endure as a sect is a testimony not only to the courage which animated them, but to the quality of their leadership. This was the greatest crisis the infant Church had had to meet. With all the unanimity of tradition to go by, with all such evidence that a dominating personal inspiration must have been in their midst, need it be questioned that the leader was Peter?

Peter would be in his seventies now. Amid the city's broken stones, amid the tumult of rebuilding, by wasted temple and echoing circus under the sheltering night, he may be conceived as moving from point to point of Christian harbourage, feeding the "flock of God" with spiritual food and encouraging it to physical consolidation. Christians could have asked no more than to hold fast to his consecrated person. So, perhaps all unconsciously, surrounded by the yet lingering reek of fire and blood, Peter the fisherman fulfilled the destiny decreed for him. "Thou art Peter and upon this rock I will build my Church; and the gates of hell shall not prevail against it."

> And I saw as it were a sea of glass mingled with fire: and them that had gotten the victory over the beast, and over his image, and over his mark, and over the number of his name, stand on the sea of glass, having the harps of God. . . . And after these things I heard a great voice of much people in heaven saying Alleluia! Salvation and glory and honour and power unto the Lord our God; for true and righteous are his judgments; for he hath judged the great whore which did corrupt the earth with her fornication, and hath avenged the blood of his servants at her hand. And again they said Alleluia!

Thus wrote the author of Revelation within measurable years of A.D. 64.

9

The Darkening Scene

UNDER October stars Jerusalem, the Holy City, lies asleep. Their crystal glancings touch forms of leaf and branch on roofs where grottoes have been made for the Festival of Tabernacles. Within these arbours children breathe softly in their slumber. Along narrow ways down below the city guard paces quietly. On high the Temple police stand silhouetted against the blue night, resting on their massive staves. From the parapet of Antonia a sparkle responds to the luminous sky as a sentry, turning, swings his spear. Tents and coniferous latticings cover the lower slopes of the tranquil Mount of Olives where pilgrims are encamped. Peace prevails; but it is an uneasy peace, for the land is compassed with fear and foreboding.

Suddenly the silence is broken by a voice, a shrill lamentation that has begun to haunt the streets by day and night: "Woe, woe to Jerusalem! A voice from the east, a voice from the west, a voice from the four winds! A voice against Jerusalem and the Temple, against the bridegroom and the bride, against the whole people! Woe, woe!"

The children under their leafy canopies turn restlessly; their elders awaken and listen and are chilled. The Temple guards hurry to move on this prophet of doom; the Roman sentry grins at these melancholy, benighted Jews.

"Woe to the city and the Temple!"

It was a rustic named Jesus who roamed the ways, uttering these dismal words. He baffled the authorities by his persistence. Not a day passed but he raised his direful proclamation, and men felt that it expressed their own apprehension of impending catastrophe. The poor wretch was beaten, but he made no complaint nor asked for clemency. So soon as he was freed he staggered on, bearing his wounds and crying again, "Woe to Jerusalem!" At length he was brought before Albinus, the Roman governor, who ordered him to be scourged. Under this terrible torture—imposed by a flail with weighted thongs—the flesh was torn from his body so that his bones protruded; yet all that came from his broken voice was the same cry, "Woe to Jerusalem!" When Albinus asked him who he was and whence he came he made no coherent answer. So, having shattered his mortal frame, the governor pronounced him mad and let him go. He went, but all the city continued to hear his warning— "A voice from the east, a voice from the west"—and trembled.

They had other reason to tremble, for there was even more blood in the gutters now. The rapacious Albinus had proved a bad governor, dealing in bribe and hush-money and playing off rival High Priests and their parties, who fought one another in the streets. And news from Rome in A.D. 65 filled Albinus with fresh bitterness. Again it was the endlessly scheming Poppaea Sabina who initiated evil. Her dearest friend in Rome was a woman of like mind and habit named Cleopatra, rich, voluptuous, and unprincipled. Poppaea persuaded Nero to nominate Cleopatra's husband, Gessius Florus, as governor of Judaea by way of reward for his wife's devotion. Albinus heard the tidings that he was about to be recalled, and cynically decided to make the most of what time remained to him and to leave his successor with aggravated problems. He opened the jails in the province, executed the most notorious criminals, but let all the rest go free on payment of suitable ransoms. Great numbers of depraved and brutal men roamed Judaea, and their idle ranks were swollen immediately afterwards when, Herod's reconstructed Temple having been completed, eighteen thousand workmen were dismissed to wander the streets, join robber groups, and indulge in plunder.

It was useless to look to the puppet king Agrippa for solace or remedy. Alarmed by the decay setting in everywhere, he had more or less withdrawn from Jerusalem and had made Caesarea Philippi, in the north, his place of residence. He was building extensions to the city and had renamed it Neronias, in honour of the Emperor. Rumour said he was preparing it as a place of retreat against the final disaster to Jerusalem.

Only one conclusion can be reached about the policy Gessius Florus pursued when he arrived. Apart from making full use of opportunities to feather his own nest, which he did by wholesale exactions, penalizing villages and casting their inhabitants out of their property, he seems to have bent his considerable energies on aggravating the general situation. His aim was, apparently, to precipitate revolution in the hope of valuable plunder. Unless this be conceded it is difficult to judge his actions as other than those of a half-wit. Wherever trouble smouldered he fanned it—and trouble smouldered in all directions. Nobody knows whether he had been given specific instructions to be harsh with the Jews, but his provocations were on a scale that made people even regret the departure of the ill-tempered Albinus. He encouraged the bloody divisions in the priesthood and the city, ignored the increasing outrages of the *sicarii*, and, with irresponsible impetuosity, laid waste whole districts of the province where he conceived himself to have been offended or whence his coffers could be weighted.

The high-spirited Jews, caught up in various nationalistic movements, among which the Zealots began to play a leading part, were not slow to react as Florus presumably intended them to do. They expressed their contempt for him openly. From being a people comparatively acquiescent in their subjugation they became a people burning with zeal for revenge. Their handicap was the jealousy and bitterness among competing sects which boiled up in mortal clashes between Jew and Jew. This internal dissension was, of course, a pleasing sight to the unscrupulous governor: it would ensure chaos when the time came for open war.

When informed that the long-suffering Jews of Caesarea were about to organize an attack on the Greeks in the city Florus tactfully moved to Sebaste so that the ensuing riots could run their course. But the great Jewish rebellion was really touched-off in Jerusalem itself. The governor sent a peremptory demand for a very large sum from the sacred money of the Temple— that is, the money subscribed by Jews in all parts of the world for the maintenance of their religious institutions. The levy, said Florus, was required "for Caesar's use." His arrogance raised passion to fever-heat. He was publicly cursed and mocked. All this provided a pretext for more menacing action, and the governor was quick to take it. At the head of a substantial military force he marched into Jerusalem. In spite of their anger, the citizens, influenced to some extent by the alarmed priests and Levites, who ran about covered in ashes beseeching them not to enrage Rome, offered no armed resistance. That did not save them. Having established himself in the Herodian palace, Florus ordered his troops to plunder the upper market and put to death any who dared to oppose them.

The Roman garrison in Judaea did not consist of legionary troops—that is, troops of the regular Imperial army. It was composed of auxiliaries, or colonial levies. From such formations the soldiers who crucified Jesus must have been drawn. They were recruited mainly out of Samaria, and, as Samaritans, they harboured a traditional enmity towards the Jew, so that, when occasion offered, they were unsparing in their bitterness. This pass proved no exception. They sacked all the region of the market enthusiastically, and were merciless towards those who lived there. While some were crucified and others scourged, the majority were put to the sword. More than three thousand men, women, and children died. Thereafter the situation deteriorated rapidly into guerrilla war.

Berenice, Agrippa's incestuous and sometimes remorseful sister, was in Jerusalem at the time, fulfilling a religious vow. Her beautiful hair had been cut off as part of this observance. In a last loyal display towards her people she presented herself before Florus, barefoot and clad only in a coarse chemise, pleading with him to stay his hand. She was dismissed abruptly, and, indeed, found herself imperilled by the wrath of wider conflict all around, so that she took the earliest opportunity of leaving the city.

In the riotous days that followed the Jews, realizing that Florus's intention was to capture the Temple and seize its treasures, destroyed the terrace and portico by which it was linked to the Tower of Antonia, the Roman fortress. Thereupon the governor himself withdrew from the city with his ineffective soldiery. Having stimulated resentment into open rebellion, he informed his superior, the Imperial legate at Antioch, Cestius Gallus, of the perilous state of affairs. Cestius Gallus was a man singularly attuned to the governor's methods, sharing a similar rapacious temperament. They were friends, and also, it seems, fellow-conspirators in the business of inflaming Palestine. Conditions rapidly worsened. Agrippa arrived, endeavoured to pacify the Jews, failed, and retired once more to the north; but shortly afterwards he sent three or four thousand troops ostensibly to protect the Temple. They were attacked by one or other of the nationalist brigades that were by now building up their formations and improving their armament.

Malignancy flared up everywhere. In the Greek-speaking cities such as Caesarea the Jewish inhabitants were massacred. By retaliation the Hebrews throughout Peraea and in Syria butchered their Gentile neighbours. Powerful rival leaders such as Eleazar and Manahem emerged, adding war among the Jews themselves to the general confusion. Then totally unexpected shocks fell on the Romans. Their stronghold near the Dead Sea was captured—a castle named Massada—but worse was to follow. After a two-day assault Jewish insurgents broke into the Tower of Antonia itself, driving out the Roman garrison, which fled to the Herodian palace. Abandoned by Florus and surrounded by a massive and enraged enemy, the remnant fought desperately, but in the end they had to surrender. Vile treachery illustrates the depth to which hatred had now sunk. These Roman prisoners, having been induced to lay down their arms, were slaughtered to a man.

This was the moment for which Florus and Cestius Gallus had waited. Nobody could now dispute that strong, warlike measures were required to deal with so grave a revolutionary outbreak. From his headquarters at Antioch Cestius marched south with a powerful army. With him he had the Twelfth Legion, several cohorts of additional infantry, some regiments of horse and auxiliaries supplied by allied Arabian kinglings—altogether over twenty thousand men. Bloody engagements were fought in Galilee and along the southern plain, but his resolve was to press

on to Jerusalem in order to kill the revolt at its heart and, no
doubt, glut himself and his friend Florus with the spoils. Nor
did the citizens hide their dismay when they awoke to find this
formidable Roman army drawn up on Mount Scopus overlook-
ing Jerusalem. Chaos prevailed inside the walls while Cestius
Gallus waited, suspending his attack for three days in the hope
of a profitable surrender.

It was certainly about this time, and it may well have been
during this ominous pause before the final storm, that the Christians of Jerusalem decided to leave. Prophecy coloured their
thought and dictated their actions. They had watched unrest
grow from bitterness to turmoil and battle. Daily they heard
the poor rustic crying his dismal message: "A voice from the
east! A voice from the west! Woe to Jerusalem and the
Temple!" When they met they listened to other words spoken
by Jesus and retold by the elders who had heard him utter
them: "When ye shall see the abomination of desolation,
spoken of by Daniel the prophet, stand in the holy place, then
let them which be in Judaea flee into the mountains." Or, as
another version says more explicitly: "And when ye shall see
Jerusalem compassed with armies, then know that the desolation thereof is nigh. Then let them which are in Judaea flee to
the mountains."

There on Mount Scopus, upon the holy place, preparing to
attack the Temple of God, compassing them with destruction,
stood the Roman army. From the roof-top of their meeting-
place, from the Temple courts, they looked up and saw the
implacable legionaries in full war kit, each man with his oblong
shield and spear, his sword, his axe, his faggot and leather, the
summer sun flashing on breastplate and helmet. It was time to
go. The hour was at hand. Faith would guide their steps. Their
prayers were profound as they made hurried preparation.
Danger would beset them at every turn, for each man's hand was
set against his neighbour now. It must have been with heavy
hearts that these Jewish Christians left the Holy City of their
fathers, left the Temple where their Messiah had preached, cast
farewell glances towards the Mount of Olives and the clumps
of cypress that marked the Garden of Gethsemane, and,

through some sable night, perhaps in scattered groups so as not to attract attention, skirted the Jericho road and turned their faces to the north.

High skill must have been shown by their leader, Simeon, the cousin of Jesus, for they seem to have made their escape without being checked or attacked by Zealot bands, revolutionary forces, Temple thugs, or Roman sentries—and all such were alert in those brief days and nights on the eve of battle. In the persons of these refugees the Church of Christ was abandoning Jerusalem as its headquarters for ever. As they took the rocky by-paths leading over the hills to Peraea, listening for pursuers or the iron ring of Imperial patrols, they can hardly have realized the history they were making. But they knew this was their Master's wish. "He was despised and rejected; a man of sorrows and acquainted with grief." So it must be with them until the day-star shone again. "Fear not, little flock, for it is your father's good pleasure to give you the kingdom."

They found their way to Pella, a town in the Decapolis, beyond the control of Jewry or of Florus, and there they settled. We have no information about the persons who composed this community, but it is safe to assume that Simeon continued to preside over them and reasonable to expect that some of those who had known Jesus would be with them. At this time Peter was in Rome, John was at Ephesus or elsewhere in Asia, Paul, released by Nero's judges, was continuing his missions oversea. There is support for the tradition that the disciple Andrew went to Asia and Thomas is said to have gone to Parthia, but there is little weight about this. Mystery veils the fate of the rest of the Twelve—Matthew, Philip, Bartholomew, Simon the Zealot, Thaddaeus, and James (the son of Alphaeus). Later tidings were to come of Jude's family, indicating that they remained true to the faith, but of these others no murmur echoes from the past. That some of them went to Pella, or maintained close links with the sect there, is probable.

What kind of life did they live? They would have to work, each according to his trade, for though no doubt alms continued to come from the European churches and those in Asia Minor, it is difficult to believe they came as abundantly as they would have done to Jerusalem. Their worship would be simple and devout, intertwined with Jewish rites; but there are indications that the Eucharist was practised in primitive form. To judge from the earliest references, it would seem that they rose at dawn, sang a hymn, and then ate a common meal before which the cup and the bread were blessed in remembrance of the Last Supper. Prayers followed; petitions were made in the name of Jesus Christ; and the "Amen" was said.

Although Christianity had won a considerable following in Jerusalem, it can hardly be that all of them, or even the majority, went to Pella. Ordinary laymen would have their families to consider, their trade to follow, their shops to keep, in spite of the city's tribulation. It would appear, therefore, that in the main it was what we would call the 'ministry' that departed—the leaders, deacons, and those who had abandoned earthly things and given their lives to the cause. For this reason the hypothesis may well be advanced that Pella harboured a unique body of discipleship; and it is likely that in its quiet ways the earliest efforts were made to put the sayings of Jesus into writing. Hitherto, with so many actual witnesses of his life and teaching—for it must not be forgotten that, in addition to the Twelve, several scores of lesser followers had been commissioned to preach the Word—reliance had been placed on memory. Modern man has lost the art of accurate recollection and repetition; but in times when writing was a scarce and difficult luxury this was a custom invested with integrity. That is why close attention must be paid to what is known as 'oral tradition'—word of mouth—stemming from antiquity. Honourable men, even over long periods, told the news more correctly than many a newspaper to-day.

But the realization that time was passing, that the men who, as adults, had listened to Jesus were growing old—in their seventies or late sixties—added to the upheaval caused by the removal from Jerusalem and the further possible dispersion implicit in it; all this must have emphasized the desirability of committing his teaching to a more durable form lest it became hazy or distorted.

No literature has been so exhaustively subjected to scholarly analysis as the four Gospels, and while there are various theories concerning them there is wide agreement that they must have been preceded by some other Gospel, or collection of sayings, that has disappeared. Similarity in phrase and other clues make the assumption convincing. This lost record is known to Biblical scholarship as Q (from *Quelle*, or source). Our existing Gospels, though written independently, seem either to have depended on Q for some of their content or to have been amended in the light of Q. The earliest is St Mark, which was composed at Rome about A.D. 67, apparently under the direct inspiration and with the consent of Peter himself. Whether Mark had already in his possession a copy of Q, or whether his work received later additions from Q, we do not know. Whether Q was written in Greek or Aramaic—the Hebrew variant spoken by the common people of Galilee and Judaea, and, of course, by Jesus—is also unprovable. But it is not unreasonable to suppose that, if it originated in Palestine, it would be first put into the ordinary tongue.

Papias, who was Bishop of Hierapolis, in Asia Minor, and was personally acquainted with those who had known some of the Twelve disciples, wrote in about A.D. 130: "Matthew compiled the oracles in the Hebrew language; but every one interpreted them as he was able." At first sight this looks like a piece of offhand criticism hardly flattering to Matthew, but Papias was a clumsy writer. He speaks not about an account of Jesus's life but about "oracles." If the sentence has significance—and it is our only near-contemporary reference to Matthew—it can surely mean that Matthew put down the sayings of Christ, the "oracles," and that others used them, or "interpreted" them, according to their will. In other words, is it not a tenable theory that Matthew, the tax-collector from Capernaum, was in fact the compiler of Q, and that the Gospel which bears his name is one of the later adaptations from Q made by another hand?

The possibility cannot be dismissed that Q, if not composed earlier at Jerusalem, was assembled at Pella under the sense of urgency created by the events which dictated that move and the generally continuing threat to the original Christian band.

When they had been in their new home but a short time they

would have heard tidings that, reaching Rome, caused consternation there. After having waited irresolutely for a week Cestius Gallus suddenly ordered a general assault on Jerusalem. The main attack by the Twelfth Legion was on the north side of the Temple. Repelled in this, the Romans reformed, building a *testudo*, or pyramid of shields, and they had almost broached an entry in spite of the frenzied resistance of the Jews when Cestius inexplicably called them off and ordered a general retreat.

The Jews hastened in pursuit, pouring out of the city, and in the course of a few days, having driven the Roman army into open flight, they brought it to condign defeat. In the pass of Bethoron the Romans were ambushed and trapped by many thousands of their enemies. Only nightfall saved them from decimation. Under cover of darkness, and through the heroism of the rearguard, many, including Cestius, escaped. They were chased to Antipatris in their headlong flight towards Caesarea. Nearly six thousand Romans died. This was the greatest disaster that had befallen Imperial arms for over half a century. Rome was shaken and shamed; Judaea was no longer under its control.

IO

The Emperor's Choice

POPPAEA was dead. Life had given her thirty-five years, therefore she died in the full June of her days, when experience adds confident vivacity to beauty yet flourishing and completes a woman's glory. It is a cruel moment in which to be cut down, yet who would mourn Poppaea? A murderess and a deceiver, having no love to give yet being so outwardly lovable, what tears need be shed for her? She died of a miscarriage, brought about, it is said, by a kick from her husband because she reproached him for neglecting her. Mercy may well have decided that no unhappy child should be born of such a union.

The lamentations of Nero were ostentatious, prolonged, and blubbery, becoming indeed almost a public nuisance. Since grief deeply felt is dumb, and sorrow clothes itself in silence, his protestations, shrine-building, and oily declamations may more justly be ascribed to Thespian conceit than to the soul's agony. In this affair, as in others, he had to act the part, and, being unprofessional, he overacted. Poppaea's body was embalmed; it was not cremated.

But mourning, which became Nero so little, had at last to give way to the compelling needs of Art. The long-cherished visit to Greece was realized. In September A.D. 66 the Emperor, accompanied by an enormous retinue, which included Tigellinus and Sporus, set off for the purer air and more worthy inspirations of the Athenian land. He was welcomed rapturously, felt he had reached his spiritual home, and plunged into an orgy of song and poesy, participating in the contests and bedecking his brow with conquering chaplets.

Among a large number of distinguished Romans who had

been ordered to join his train was one to whom these lyrical excesses were a disgusting bore. Titus Flavius Vespasianus, the soldier, would certainly not have budged an inch voluntarily to accompany Nero on such a gallivant, but commands had to be obeyed. Vespasian was now in his fifty-ninth year and seems to have been in quiet retirement from the army's 'active list' when he was summoned to the Greek tour. He was a simple-living man of modest origin. His father had been a money-lender in a small provincial way of business in Italy, and it was ability alone that had carried the son to high command. His genius had shone most brilliantly in Germany and Britain, and the soldiers had an affection for him. He possessed that steady confidence in his own judgment which gives some men the capacity to inspire absolute trust in others.

Though indifferent to the more delicate points of social re-finement and *bourgeois* in habit, Vespasian had a barbed wit when he chose to use it, while as a commander in the field he was deliberate and far-seeing. But now his fighting days were apparently over, and, being vigorous both in body and mind, he was probably very much the grumbling, cynical veteran when he found himself moving about in the unsought company of Greek lyrists and rhetoricians. He took little pains to disguise his contempt for Nero's follies; therefore, when summoned to a private audience with the Emperor, he may well have concluded that he was about to receive some grim sentence of displeasure.

But Nero had a vein of uncanny shrewdness in one important field. He was an adroit judge of soldiers. No military captain himself, he was yet more perceptive than some of his advisers when it came to picking the right man for the job. Had he not chosen Corbulo to deal with the Parthians and Suetonius in so timely a fashion to meet the revolt in Britain? Now, having just received news of the dire calamity to Cestius Gallus in Palestine, he by-passed any recommendations to the contrary and sent for Vespasian. Instead of being rebuked for his Philistinism in re-gard to the arts, Vespasian was given the supreme command in Syria, with orders to bring the arrogant Jews to their knees. One can picture his delight when he left the Imperial presence; here was man's work to be done, away from all this fluting and fiddling! As for Nero, he little knew that by this decision he had nominated his successor to the purple.

With customary dispatch Vespasian laid his plans. He himself set out immediately from Greece for Antioch. At the same time he sent his son, Titus, to Alexandria to bring back two legions, the Fifth and Tenth, appointing Ptolemais, the seaport near Galilee, as their rendezvous. Vespasian collected the Fifteenth Legion at Antioch, together with a large force of auxiliaries and cavalry, and in the spring of A.D. 67 joined Titus at Ptolemais, when their combined army amounted to over fifty thousand men. In the meantime the Jews had spent the winter preparing their defences throughout Judaea and Galilee. Though still handicapped by internal feuds, with which Jerusalem in particular was distracted, there was greater unity in the land than hitherto, for men realized that a decisive war with Rome was imminent, and none underrated the skill of the great commander who had been so unexpectedly sent against them.

Too astute to repeat the mistakes of Cestius Gallus, Vespasian did not hurry towards Jerusalem. He determined first to clear his flanks and rear, and devoted the summer to overcoming Galilee. Bitter engagements were fought in which Titus distinguished himself. Towns like Jotapata and Gabara offered stern resistance and had to be carried by storm; on Mount Gerizim a bloody battle was fought. But step by step the Romans achieved the mastery, and before the year was out Tarichaea and Tiberias had capitulated. The way was open for the conquest of Peraea and, by that route, to Jerusalem.

G

The Crown of Wild Olive

VESPASIAN had a nephew living in Rome, Flavius Clemens. Some thirty years later he was to die the death of a Christian martyr. It is believed that the introduction of the faith into his home was due to a freedman in his service who, according to custom, bore his patron's name. The freedman was Clement, or, as he is known to history, Clement of Rome, one of the great Apostolic Fathers. According to this reconstruction, suggested by Lightfoot, Clement was probably of Jewish origin, for his writings betray a Hebraic knowledge of the Old Testament. At the time when Nero went to Greece he might have been about thirty years old.

By now Clement was one of the more energetic figures among the Christians of the capital, working under Peter. Another was Linus, a man of maturer age. Little is known about Linus, but his name suggests a humble birth like that of Clement. Both these men were intimates of the two great Apostles, Peter and Paul, and both were to become bishops of Rome. They appear to have lived through the fire and the terror. Clement's own words, testifying to the sufferings of "a great multitude of the elect," are set down in a manner which, though not explicit, leads to the belief that he was an eyewitness. Both men must have been familiar with Mark, Luke, Silvanus, Timothy, and others who came and went on the Church's business, and they obviously played an outstanding part in the work of reconstruction after Nero's persecution, otherwise it would be difficult to justify their later eminence.

To men of their generation, as to the younger Christians in Pella, there seemed to be one pressing need. As they listened to the revered Peter, in candle-lighted catacomb or behind closed curtains, they realized the responsibility that would fall on them when he and the other elders were gone; for even men like Mark were now middle-aged. They and their contemporaries pressed for a written account of the life of Jesus; that it should be done while Peter was able to supervise it—Peter who had known all those things that had happened on the Galilean shore and at Jerusalem. Mark joined his voice to theirs and undertook the task.

From the traditions it seems that Peter was not very enamoured of the idea to begin with. Papias, writing some sixty years afterwards, says Peter "used to adapt his instructions to the needs of the moment, not with a view to putting together the Dominical oracles." The old disciple would probably feel that it was not for him to sanction what his Master had not done himself. Moreover, the first Christians lived in hourly expectation of Christ's return and did not feel any need to worry about posterity. Nevertheless, Mark's Gospel was done. Papias says: "He kept a single aim in view; not to omit anything of what he heard, nor to state anything therein falsely." This testimony can be relied on because Papias was in close association with the Fathers and would almost certainly have known Mark's younger friends personally—could even have met Mark in his youth. Simon Peter was pleased with the result and is said to have authorized the book to be read in the Church.

The last year or so of the Apostle's life bequeathed all that he left of his mind in script—the First Epistle of Peter and the oversight of the Gospel according to St Mark. Who could have done more? Now the end had come, his work was over. "Simon, son of Jonas . . . when thou wast young thou girdedst thyself and walkedst whither thou wouldest; but when thou shalt be old thou shalt stretch forth thy hands and another shall gird thee and carry thee whither thou wouldest not."

The other that girded him (if the sequence here propounded is correct) was Claudius Helius, who had been left in charge of the government in Rome by Nero. Acting of necessity under him, the city authorities must have decided that Peter was a dangerous stirrer-up of trouble, a significant "enemy of the human race"; and it came to the ears of the Christians that the

old man's death had been decreed. For this version of his end we
have to rely on an early legend, extracting from its fictitious
embellishments anything that bears the mark of trustworthy
oral tradition. It is told in a document known as the *Acts of
Peter*. No reliance can be placed on the details of the tale, but
a broad outline of what happened may well be interpreted from
it.

According to this story, the Prefect of the City and his friends
were newly inflamed against the fugitive Christians because
their wives and mistresses had been influenced by them. The
women had been persuaded to abandon their paramours and
live chaste lives, largely owing to Peter himself. In particular
the legend names Xanthippe, a woman of excelling beauty. It
was she who, discovering the plot to kill Peter, warned the
Christian community. They pleaded with the old man to flee
and save his life so that he might continue to serve the Lord.
Then comes the famous episode of *Quo vadis?* Peter decided to
leave Rome in disguise:

> And he obeyed the brethrens' voice and went forth alone . . .
> and as he went forth out of the city he saw the Lord entering
> into Rome. And when he saw him he said, "Lord, whither goest
> thou?" And the Lord said unto him, "I go unto Rome to be
> crucified." And Peter said unto him, "Lord, art thou being
> crucified again?" He said unto him, "Yea, Peter, I am being
> crucified again." And Peter came to himself . . . and returned to
> Rome.

It is impossible to study this moving legend without believing
that it enshrines something of essential truth. We may reject
the preliminaries about Xanthippe and the women. We may, if
we choose, discount the picturesque vision of Christ on the
Appian Way. What remains is a simple tale of a man deciding
to run from danger, realizing that his duty is otherwise, and
then returning to face his death. This surely rings true of the
Peter we know from other sources. It brings vividly to mind his
behaviour thirty years earlier, on the morning of Christ's trial
at Jerusalem. Then, warming his hands by a brazier in the
courtyard outside where the Sanhedrin were examining Jesus, he
had denied to inquirers that he was a disciple. Thrice he had

denied it, because he was afraid. Then the cock had crowed, reminding him of his Master's prophecy, and he had gone out to stumble through the deserted streets, weeping bitterly and ashamed of himself.

Is not this the same Peter afflicted with fear—understandable, human fear—and then being overwhelmed by remorse for his weakness? The man who wept in Jerusalem in A.D. 29 was the same man who, conscience-stricken, turned back on the road from Rome in A.D. 67. He "came to himself," as the old document says, and knew that he must accept the challenge.

Peter was crucified. There is no need to reject the tradition which tells how he was nailed to the cross upside down because, humbly, he shrank from all comparison with his Redeemer. It would be like him to make such a request. Had he not been the first, long ago, to proclaim, "Thou art the Christ"? On the assumption, for which there is some cause, that he was a year or two older than Jesus, Simon Peter would be about seventy-five when he died. The precise place of execution is not known, but everything points to the locality where so many had suffered three years earlier. As Renan says, "His shade wanders ever in Christian legend about the foot of the Vatican and Nero's garden and obelisk."

But for Paul also the end was at hand. He had left Italy four years earlier, but either just before or just after the death of Peter he must have returned to Rome and was imprisoned there for a second time. It would seem that the authorities were resolved on keeping the Christians in check even if they did not indulge in another mass-murder.

Where had Paul been in the interim? There is an intriguing mystery about Spain. That he intended to go there is evident from what he had said in his Epistle to the Romans, and the possibility that he did, in fact, visit the country emerges from a famous passage written by Clement in A.D. 95—less than thirty years after the Apostle's death. This is what Clement wrote in the course of a letter to the Church at Corinth:

> But to cease from the examples of old time, let us come to those who contended in the days nearest to us; let us take the noble examples of our own generation. Through jealousy and

envy the greatest and most righteous pillars of the Church were persecuted, and contended unto death. Let us set before our eyes the good Apostles: Peter who, because of unrighteous jealousy suffered not one or two but many trials, and having thus given his testimony, went to the glorious place which was his due. Through jealousy and strife Paul showed the way to the prize of endurance. Seven times he was in bonds, he was exiled, he was stoned, he was a herald both in the east and in the west; he gained the noble fame of his faith; he taught righteousness to all the world; and when he had reached the limits of the west he gave his testimony before the rulers, and thus passed from the world and was taken up into the Holy Place—the greatest example of endurance.

What is meant by "the limits of the west"? Could it be anything but Spain? The Peninsula represented not only the geographic limit of the then known world, but also the political limit of the Roman Empire. It is unfortunate that Clement had a certain poetical, or rhetorical, approach to writing which in this case may have masked a simple, but important, statement of fact. In the absence of other confirmation it cannot be claimed that Paul achieved his ambition by going to Spain; yet, because of this reference by Clement, it is equally impossible to dismiss the tradition that he did. Of all men Clement would know the truth, and that makes his obscurity all the more tantalizing.

If the epistles to Timothy and Titus were written by Paul it would seem that after his release in A.D. 63, whether he visited Spain or not, he certainly went once more to the East. The letter to Titus was sent from Nicopolis, in Macedonia, and the first letter to Timothy originated in Asia. There is much controversy about the authorship of these letters, and many scholars consider them to have been composed long after Paul's death. Their language and to some extent their doctrine are said to reflect later manners and thought. At the same time, the second Epistle to Timothy, written in Rome, has a strong claim to be genuine, for the persons named in it and the news about them which it contains would have little relevance or meaning if interposed by a later hand. Could a later hand, indeed, *have* interposed them? Paul had been brought before Nero's judges for the second time, and anticipated his fate in one of the most moving passages in literature: "For I am now ready to be offered and the time of my departure is at hand. I have fought a good fight, I have finished my course, I have kept the faith." These words break upon the shore of the heart like waves flowing from a sea of truth: they are not *ersatz*.

He speaks about his companions.

> For Demas hath forsaken me, having loved the present world, and is departed unto Thessalonica; Crescens to Galatia, Titus unto Dalmatia. Only Luke is with me. Take Mark and bring him with thee. . . . And Tychicus have I sent to Ephesus. The cloak that I left at Troas with Carpus, when thou comest bring with thee, and the books but especially the parchments. . . . Salute Prisca and Aquila and the household of Onesiphorus. Erastus abode at Corinth but Trophimus have I left at Miletum, sick.

Whether some parts of this epistle were interjected subsequently is open to question, but it is almost impossible that these little personal details could have been invented. The writer goes on to appeal to Timothy to visit him in Rome: "Do thy diligence to come before winter." This, coupled with the reference to Mark's being now in Asia, leads to the conjecture that Paul was writing from prison somewhere about the summer of A.D. 67. After the crucifixion of Peter in the early part of that year we may presume that Mark had gone to Ephesus, possibly with Timothy himself, and that Paul, now sensing that judgment would be passed on him in the course of a few months, wanted to see them both once more before he died.

The closing words of this epistle mention those who, in addition to Luke, were steadfast in Rome. "Eubulus greeteth thee, and Pudens, and Linus, and Claudia, and all the brethren." Here is named that Linus whom we know from independent and trustworthy sources to have become Bishop of Rome immediately after the deaths of Peter and Paul. He was the first successor of Peter in the primacy. But another name merits consideration. Who was Claudia?

An elaborate theory was formerly projected that she was a British princess who married one Pudens, but it does not stand up to investigation and is now discarded. On the other hand, the name was common only in association with the royal freedwomen. As Bishop Lightfoot comments, this Claudia "was not improbably connected with the Imperial palace." But nobody seems to have ventured a perfectly reasonable proposition—was she Claudia Acte herself, Nero's first and faithful mistress, the tender and compassionate girl from Pergamos?

John Chrysostom, writing in the fourth century, makes the definite assertion that Paul baptized one of Nero's concubines. Though this was a late statement, it is to be remembered that Chrysostom spent his life in the East—largely at Antioch and Constantinople—and a reliable tradition concerning Claudia Acte may well have been maintained in that part of the world whence, as a slave, she had originally been taken. All the hints we possess of her life—her association with the Annaea family and their Christian friends, her uncomplaining loyalty, the modesty of her character to which a Roman inscription pays tribute, her religious propensity displayed when she built a shrine to Ceres—combine to reinforce the possibility that Claudia Acte at last came into the fold of the Church. She was now in her thirtieth year.

About Paul's death there is little reliable information to depend on. Origen is emphatic that he died later than Peter, and deduction confirms this. It is also clear that the event occurred during Nero's reign; therefore it is most likely to have been in the winter or spring A.D. 67–68. He seems to have been beheaded; maybe his Roman citizenship saved him from a more despicable end on the cross. From ancient times legend has put his burial-place on the Via Ostia; nobody in fact knows. But even that brave body, though it was barely sixty years old, must have been tired after its stupendous exertions. We know that it had been afflicted by chronic illness beside the beatings and privations to which it had been subjected. Of all men this one indeed had "fought a good fight" and won an immortal crown.

Linus was now chosen to be head of the Church in Rome, sustained by Clement and the loyalty of the congregation; and it was at the beginning of Linus's bishopric that Nero returned in triumph from Greece, putting on a spectacle that made the Roman mob delirious with joy. He had been reluctant to come back, and his deputy Helius had had to go and fetch him; for affairs in Rome were not propitious and already the first mutterings of revolt were to be heard in the provinces of the Empire.

Nero entered his capital as a conqueror of the arts, driving in the triumphal chariot which Augustus Caesar had used to mark more enduring feats. He was clad in a purple robe over which flowed an outer cloak glittering with golden stars. On his head he wore a crown of wild olive to symbolize his Olympian achievements. A gorgeous procession accompanied him through vast cheering crowds. Intoxicated by all this, he had little inclination, either then or in the following months, to bother about sinister news stemming from beyond the Alps and the seas.

But Vindex in Gaul, Galba in Spain, Otho in Lusitania, and Vitellius—proconsuls of the Empire facing sterner realities than Nero acknowledged—were in their several ways considering how to bring about his downfall and, additionally, either their own self-interest or vengeance. Hard-bitten generals, surveying their war-tested legions in the plains and defiles where Rome kept the barbarians at bay, were revolted by what they heard about the silken-robed harpist and his fabricated sensualities. To all the warnings that came to him Nero turned a deaf ear, continuing his course of feast and game, with no understanding that the crown of wild olive, conferred on him by obsequious and blatant flattery, was the only futile crown he now possessed. Swords of tougher metal than he had ever had to contemplate were out of their scabbards now, pointing Romeward.

It was only in the last week or two of life that he awakened fully to his desperate situation. The Praetorian Guard, the metropolitan legions, rose against him in favour of Galba. As the Italian sun intensified its summer heat he discovered that there could be no leisurely retreat from Rome to the sea or Campania this year. Only final retreat from glory remained. Terror seized him. His friends deserted him. He stared upon the incredible flamboyance of his palace—with its huge statue of himself in the vestibule, its pillared halls and miles of gardens —and knew that it was no longer his. Where the voice of sycophancy and the prostrate form of the toad-eater had made sweet music and pleasing genuflexion only silence and emptiness remained. The spectacle of Nero at that moment, amid the golden shell of his despised opulence, recalls the words written by the now-dead Seneca: "In no better way can God discredit what we covet than by bestowing those things on the basest men while withholding them from the best."

Nero fled—anywhere, anywhere—in the hope of keeping his life. With but a faithful slave or two to attend him, he rode out of the capital by night, holding his cloak around him lest he should be recognized by those who only a few months earlier had delighted to feast their eyes on his person. Galloping past the Praetorian barracks, he heard the soldiers shouting as they proclaimed his successor.

Shelter was offered him in the house of Phaon, a freedman, four miles out of Rome. Here he crawled on his fat stomach into a dark hiding-place. The Senate had declared him a public enemy, and a posse of the Praetorian Guard had been sent to hunt him down. Suicide alone remained. As the centurion strode towards the shadowed corner where he had crept Nero put a blade to his flabby throat and an attendant gave it the necessary shove. It was the 9th of June, A.D. 68, the sixth anniversary of the murder of his first wife, the innocent Octavia. "What an artist is lost in me!" was one of his several last phrases of lamentation.

A few days later his body, covered in robes of white and gold, was borne on a pallet to a hasty burial. There were only three mourners—two of his old nurses and the constant Claudia Acte. The brief committal followed a pagan fashion, but was there a Christian prayer on Acte's lips as she turned aside when it was over? Only the quiet air stirring the myrtles on the Pincian hill that day will ever know.

12

The Purple

POUNDING hooves and close-hauled ships made their way to Caesarea during the early months of A.D. 69. There during part of the winter Vespasian had remained, waiting. His three battle-wrought legions with their auxiliaries were poised for the final assault on Jerusalem, but no trumpet sounded the advance, no cohort moved into action. News from Rome was deciding greater issues. This news came in a sequence which, in the judgment of the commander-in-chief and his subordinates, tended in one direction. There was much coming and going and heightened excitement among them. There must have been constant discussion between men like Tiberius Alexander, the chief of staff, and the legionary generals—Sextus Cerealis of the Fifth, Lucius Lepidus of the Tenth, and Titus Frigius of the Fifteenth. The fate of the Empire was in the balance, and they knew they were in a key position to influence its destiny. The Jews could wait for their *coup de grâce*.

On Nero's death the aged Galba had seized the purple, but soon he in turn had been killed by the Praetorian Guard: he was too mean, they said. Then Otho—the gay libertine and former husband of Poppaea—had been proclaimed Emperor, only to be challenged by Vitellius, who had marched with his Rhine army on Rome. Vitellius—was Vitellius, the hoggish one, the arrogant, to govern the Empire? This thought drew a murmur from the Roman ranks in Judaea, and they looked towards their own honoured leader, greaved and buckled as a warrior should be, pacing the marbled *praetorium* at Caesarea.

In May came tidings that galvanized everything into action. Vitellius had defeated Otho's forces, Otho was dead, and Vitellius was Emperor in Rome. On the instant the army in Judaea and Syria cried aloud its own choice—*"Flavius Vespasianus Imperator!"*—and Vespasian was no longer laggard. He moved at lightning speed, descending on Egypt, accepting authority there, and forbidding the grain ships to sail to Rome. Thus he flung a stranglehold on Vitellius. Rome depended for its daily bread on the constant arrival of corn from the Nile, and the one fear of its authorities and inhabitants was that the supply should ever be halted for long. Acting now in concert with their comrades in the East, the legions from the Danube rebelled. They swept into Italy, entered Rome, put Vitellius to death, and held the city till Vespasian should arrive to be invested with the purple.

All had happened in a few months. The soldier from Reate, a typical provincial Italian, was master of the world, and men realized for the first time that noble blood was not a prerequisite for the supreme office. Would he dare to call himself Caesar? He did! One may imagine the smile on his rubicund face when he first added the title, for Vespasian was never subject to self-delusion and never lost his sense of perspective. He was now turned sixty, a bull-necked, hawk-nosed, double-chinned, bright-eyed widower, sagacious, unpretentious, but not in the least overawed by the latest turn of fortune. He took it all in his manly stride.

He lost no time in knocking down the relics of Nero's delusions, including the Golden House, which he wisely regarded as a temptation to future rulers to misjudge their mortality. He jerked the flaccid army together by imposing severe discipline, and he appointed his beloved son Titus as commander-in-chief in Judaea, with orders to expedite the subjection of Jerusalem. Titus, who had been out of the country, hastened back to Palestine to direct the war. Everywhere an invigorating spirit pulsed through the Empire's affairs.

A more engaging character than Vespasian never ruled from the Capitoline. Although he manifested the rough and, by modern standards, cruel manners of his age and profession, he was not intolerant. He inaugurated a period of tranquility in which the Christian Church grew apace. Linus, the Bishop of Rome, and his fraternity were left in peace, and thousands must

have been converted to the faith during his reign. It is doubtful
if Vespasian ever gave a thought to religion, pagan or otherwise.
He accepted the priestly offices inherent in the Principate, but
probably with an inwardly winking eye. Towards all ceremony
he had an attitude summed up in the expression "Damn nonsense!" but he acquiesced in it because he knew the political
value of tradition. He had loads of common sense.

What chuckling satisfaction he must have derived when he
assumed his serene authority in Rome! For he had been very
much out of favour during the preceding reign. A story is told
of a certain Court official who, in the time of Nero, had thrown
Vespasian from the Imperial antechamber with the remark,
"Get out—go to hell!" This unfortunate fellow was in despair
when Vespasian arrived to sit on Nero's throne, and he took the
first opportunity of grovelling before the new divinity and beseeching pardon for his former inexcusable conduct. Placidly,
Vespasian looked down on him. "Oh, go to hell!" was all he
said, and that was all the revenge exacted.

On one occasion he asked the Senate how much his Imperial
funeral would impoverish the State when, in due time, he came
to die. He was told that appropriate pomp would cost about ten
million sesterces. "All right," said Vespasian; "give me a hundred thousand now, and when I'm dead throw me in the Tiber
without any fuss." No more illiterate than he was dull, he loved
a coarse Latin joke, but he was also witty in the Greek tongue.
While he kept a watchful eye on every aspect of government
and had his Ministers, generals, and officials constantly on their
toes, he decided to make up for lost time by enjoying those
pursuits which none could now gainsay him.

He relished a well-chosen group of concubines, and yet he
seems to have had a fascination for women of different degree.
One wealthy lady became so enamoured of him that she begged
the privilege of sharing his couch. Either hard bargaining or
excessive gratification for the lady must have accompanied the
transaction, for she rewarded him with a gift of four hundred
thousand sesterces. When such a large sum was paid over it
presented a book-keeping problem for the palace accountant. He
waited on the Emperor.

"How am I to enter this in the Imperial ledger?" he asked. "For the seduction of Vespasian," was the prompt answer.

If there is no point at which this worldly, practical, good-natured man made a positive impact on Christianity it could well be argued that, by default itself, his was a wholly beneficent influence. His very disinterest gave the churches throughout the Empire that quietude they needed to consolidate themselves. By now the earliest pattern of Church government was emerging. Degree came gradually to be defined; episcopal authority began to be modestly conceded. Bishoprics were established where councils of presbyters had hitherto run affairs, and the idea of Apostolic succession lent power and veneration to the heads of the greater communities.

Apart from Rome and Corinth, vitality was in the East—in Asia and Syria. Antioch held the precedence. It had a tradition second only to Jerusalem, for it was in Antioch that the earliest refugees and missionaries had founded a community soon after the Resurrection. Herod Antipas's foster-brother, Manaen, had been one of them. The name 'Christian' had first been used there, and the great Apostles had sojourned there.

Peter appears to have presided over the Antiochene church at some time before he went to Rome, and the Bishop of Antioch in Vespasian's reign, Evodius, claimed his authority by direct succession from the disciple. Next in importance came Ephesus, where the church had been founded by Paul and where in Vespasian's time the disciple John was living, possibly in the company of his old friend Andrew.

At Smyrna, Hierapolis, and Philadelphia episcopal sees were created, and though there is no precise evidence, it is likely that their bishops were inducted, if not always by those known to us as disciples of Jesus, by some from that larger number of lesser personal disciples whose names have not been recorded. Of these we know two—the Elder John and Aristion—who are mentioned by Papias. It has been powerfully argued by Canon Streeter that Aristion is the same person as the Ariston who is listed as the first Bishop of Smyrna. In that event the church at Smyrna was supervised by a man who had known Jesus in the flesh. There, or at Ephesus, was born into a Christian family during the first

year of Vespasian's reign a boy who was given the name Polycarp. At the same time, five or six hundred miles away at
Antioch, a well-to-do young man called Ignatius was living a
vigorous—and probably abandoned—life according to Graeco-
Roman custom.

These two were destined to meet once before each laid down
his life for the Christ.

13

The Power and the Glory

WHEN the morning sun cleared the Jordan ranges men staring on Jerusalem from a distance had to shade their eyes from the glare of the Temple. Its nine gates, covered with beaten silver, its Eastern front plated with solid gold, threw back the rays intensified so that the whole vast edifice flamed like a defiant jewel above the crowded city. And when the sun set in milder beams over the lonely road to Emmaus, and the fires of the day were banked, men on the hills of Benjamin saw the Temple as the habitation of a more tranquil God, lovely and pale and cloistered, all white marble, rosy-budded. So it looked afar in the summer of A.D. 70. But, in fact, the Temple now stood on top of a city stinking of death in all her ways, where only the frenzy of desperation beat in men's blood-starved veins. Jerusalem the golden, once more compassed about with armies, lay in the cup of doom, a helpless prey to famine, pestilence, and the Roman eagle.

The best of her sons had fought heroically, sallying forth often to do battle with Titus's legions in efforts to break the deadly grip he had clamped round the city. And though his great engines and pounding-rams had broken down the outer walls, his soldiers had been repulsed again and again when they tried to enter, so that Roman pride itself was shrouded in Jewish dust. By day the noise of battle still echoed among the brown hills. The trumpets rang, the serried shields of advancing cohorts trembled beneath avalanches of stones and lent a fearful drumming to the air; clashing blades interposed a sharper, deadlier note; cries of pain and fury intermingled; and all the time, from dawn to sundown, came the insistent thunder of the battering-rams, the roar of falling masonry, the splintering of timber.

The Roman could not hack his way in, the Jew could not

hack his way out. But the Jew was dying for lack of food, and Jehovah gave no answer to his prayer. Brave men had ventured forth by night to gather the carob and edible herbs, but few came back. Most of them hung now, putrefying carcases, on hundreds of crosses that covered the lower slopes around the city. Titus's soldiers had a joke about these ghastly fields of crucifixion. They said there was more timber than there was room left to plant another cross. This was the agonizing sight that met the sick eyes of the widows and fatherless when they looked forth. On what cross was their loved one nailed, rotting blasphemously before the face of the Lord?

Inside the city depraved and cowardly excesses stained the white record of self-sacrifice. Conscience does not live in criminal minds, and your murderer is rarely courageous. Jerusalem was riddled with the offscourings of the prisons and stews let loose upon the land by men like Albinus and Gessius Florus. These were little concerned about fighting the Romans, but, as famine deepened, they were very concerned about their own bellies. Wherever they suspected a crust of bread to be found they slew or tortured to get it. Indescribable torments were inflicted on those who were thought to know where food was kept. These creatures lived on rapine and plunder while their fellow-countrymen manned the shuddering walls against the common foe. Jerusalem was rotten within and implacably surrounded without. And even yet, until he was killed by a stone from a Roman catapult, the poor broken rustic wandered the mourning ways crying, "A voice from the East, a voice from the West! Woe to Jerusalem!"

Woe indeed! As each night brought its comparative lull while both armies staunched their wounds and prepared for the next day's combat, the besieged looked out on the great towers and banks which Titus was moving ever closer to them. They saw his watch-fires burning all about Mount Scopus and the Mount of Olives, down to the brook Kedron and near the pool of Siloam. How long could the end be delayed? How could they muster the strength to resist unless food and succour came to them? And whence could they expect those blessings in a pitiless world?

H

As the situation grew more desperate women and children and the aged were gathered in their thousands in the Temple courts. The Temple was a very rock of strength, a citadel in itself, and none, it was felt, dare desecrate the House of the Lord. In this steadfast place they waited for deliverance. But it must have been a dire shock to them and their defenders when it was realized that, instead of continuing to seek entry at weaker points, Titus was moving against the old Imperial fortress, the Tower of Antonia, which stood at one corner of the Temple buildings.

The Roman engines got to work, beating and riving at the massive walls which were at once foundations for the Tower and an outer rampart to the city itself. From within the Jews began countermining, their object apparently being to bring down mountains of obstructive rubble if once a real breach was made. Attempts to scale the Temple heights failed, but a temporary lodgment was effected at some point where the Antonia parapet had been broken by a ram. Here, after hand-to-hand fighting, the Romans were ejected. But under cover of night the full strength of the Fifth Legion seems to have been deployed for a carefully prepared surprise assault.

That legion's standard-bearer, two dismounted cavalrymen, and a trumpeter made their way secretly either to the Antonia breach or to some other point by way of diversion—the account given by Josephus is obscure. In cloak-and-dagger style they killed Jewish sentries, signals were sounded by the trumpeter, and the Fifth Legion moved according to prearranged strategy, probably making feint lunges to deceive the defenders. Titus may well have led them in person, for the next day he was with his victorious soldiers in possession of the fortress. It had been a night of merciless bloodshed. The Jews had fought fanatically, contesting every inch, and casualties had been very heavy on both sides.

Mastery of the Tower of Antonia gave the Romans mastery of the Temple itself. For that very purpose the Tower had been erected—to provide a strategic position dominating the heart of Judaism. The Jews were under no illusion concerning the straits in which they were now placed, and the Romans realized that at last they were in a commanding position. Titus called a council of war. His legionary generals agreed with him that the Temple must be captured, for it symbolized Jewish independence, but that it must not be destroyed. Its survival under the eagles would be an ornament to the sovereignty of Rome. They failed to understand what this emblem of Jehovah, this holy place, meant to the Jews, the chosen of God. Ferocious counter-attacks were launched by the Jewish soldiers, and in the days following the Temple courts and precincts were the scene of violent battle. Blood swamped the pavements; the corpses were piled in the marbled halls.

Lamentation rose in wild cries from the women and children when the outer gates were set on fire. Their silver coverings ran molten about the burned flesh of their defenders. As these retreated under relentless onslaughts from the garrison of the Tower fresh regiments of Roman infantry scaled the eastern and northern walls, leaping down to attack the flanks of the enemy. Showers of arrows darkened the air and hails of stones crashed against armour and masonry. Round the great altar itself, whence sacrifice to the Lord had risen in a perpetual pyre of worship, the carnage was at its worst. The hatred of years met in frantic grapple and became itself a terrible sacrifice of agony and death. Over all rolled the smoke from the developing fires, blinding friend and foe alike. Huddled women and their little ones were struck down by sword and spear or perished in the flames.

When night fell Titus, bewildered by the catastrophe that was imminent, called a halt. Whether his orders were strict enough or whether he grasped the enormity of the pending event none can judge. It is said that he expressly forbade any further destruction of the Temple fabric. But during the night desperate fighting broke out again, and he was called from his bed to witness a scene unparalleled in history. Maddened by the adamantine bitterness of the Jewish defenders, Roman infantry swept across the courts, casting flaming brands indiscriminately through arch and on roof.

At the heart of the several colonnades, courts, and pavements, beyond the altar, stood an isolated building, the sacred Temple itself. This contained the innermost sanctuary, the soul of Israel, where, in the Holy of Holies—a silent and empty chamber beyond the coloured Veil—the spirit of the Lord God visited his people. None but the most sanctified could approach beyond the ornate low wall with which it was surrounded. It was inviolate. Yet in the midst of this night of tumult, this night of flame and sword, a Roman soldier perpetrated a deed the consequences of which still beat menacingly on the fabric of our own time. He was just a common soldier, like a soldier careless, but in this hour a prey to insensate fury. In his roughened hand he carried a blazing torch—some crude stump soaked in pitch or oil. While the battle raged around him he clambered on a comrade's shoulder, to mount level with the approaching steps, and hurled his brand through the golden doorway into the Holy Place.

In a minute or two the building was on fire. The dwelling of the Most High, polluted beyond redemption, clothed itself in acrid smoke and licking flame, while the paralysed children of Israel looked on, appalled.

It was over. The end had come. It was only left to die. They threw themselves on the enemy, laying their lacerated bodies in sheaves of faithful harvest about the sacred spot. The priests and Levites clung to the scorching walls; they climbed to the roof, tearing up the thousand golden pinnacles with which it was covered and dashing them down into the Roman faces below. A number of these bearded figures fell beneath well-aimed spears into the fiery cauldron below, till the whole building collapsed.

Its fall marked the end of hope for the Jews and the triumph of Titus. When the Veil of the Temple crumbled in ashes that night so did the nationhood (though not the faith) of Israel. But desperate resistance continued in the Upper City, where the two Jewish leaders, Simon Bar Giora and John of Gischala, had retreated. In the weeks that followed more ramparts and battering-rams were brought into operation by Titus; the stubbornness of the defenders encouraged the Roman soldiery to bloody excesses. When at last they broke into the Hebrew positions they murdered, plundered, and burnt indiscriminately, and it was amid horrifying acts of violence that Jerusalem at last capitulated on September 8, A.D. 70. Old men, old women, and the weak were put to death on the spot. Younger men and women were sent into slavery or set aside for massacre by gladiators. Simon Bar Giora and hundreds of the handsomest of the remaining warriors were kept for display in the pending triumph at Rome.

Determined to stamp out any possibility of further revolt, Titus then ordered the destruction of the city. Houses and public buildings were razed to the ground. Pavements were torn up and scattered. Only a small segment of the wall was left as a defence for the Roman garrison. Three towers of Herod's palace were kept intact, rising gauntly among the acres of smoking rubble in symbol of the grandeur that had once been before it challenged Imperial Rome. By the end of the year all that remained of the Holy City was a confusion of broken masonry, bereft of human life, over which, from their encampment on Mount Scopus, the Tenth Legion kept watch and ward. The wolf and the hyaena foraged by night through this mountain of decay where mighty kings and governors had once driven in state and a rich priesthood had held pompous sway.

Little imagination is needed to realize what this catastrophe meant to the Christian refugees at Pella, across the Jordan. Surely Christ's prophecy had been fulfilled with awful completeness! Need it be doubted that brave spirits among them slipped across the intervening hills when it was dark and from some high ridge gazed down upon the blackened and silent desolation that they had known as Jerusalem, the golden, the shining, the many-tongued? Their tremulous lips framed words their Master had spoken: "See ye not all these things? Verily I say unto you, there shall not be left here one stone upon another that shall not be thrown down." If there were glory in such deeds, then the glory belonged to Titus; but whose was the power?

Young scouts from another group of refugees must also have flitted among the hills of this saddened land by night. They too had to elude Roman patrols; they too had to creep away to distant retreats before daybreak. But they were interested not so much in Jerusalem as in the wilderness to the south and east, where, from Ramat Rachel and Bethlehem, begin those ancient folds of civilization that run towards Jericho. They were survivors of the Qumrun sect of Essenes whose great settlement on the shore of the Dead Sea had been sacked and burned by the vengeful Romans.

On and off for nearly two hundred years this religious community had dwelt in the neighbourhood of Qumrun. Its members led a monastic, ritual life. Cut off from pollution by the sinful world, they studied and interpreted the Hebrew Scriptures within their isolated enclosure. They practised baptism, perfected orders of seniority and priesthood, and became an important factor in that upsurge of Messianic expectation amid which Christianity had been born. Christianity itself, with its warmth and happiness, its compassion for "publicans and sinners," and its focus on the human person of Jesus, was in the event far removed from Essenism; but there can be little doubt that Christ and his followers were fully aware of the movement, and it may be that John the Baptist, the lone prophet, was partly influenced by it.

Vespasian and Titus purged the land of all such sources of Jewish religious nationalism, and the Qumrun monastery had been attacked and destroyed by the Tenth Legion during mopping-up operations before the final assault on Jerusalem. How many of its members fled to safety and how many were butchered cannot be guessed; but in their desperation when they saw the cohorts approaching they tried to preserve their most precious documents, placing some of them in caves. There they remained, hidden not only from the Tenth Legion, but from all mankind, until in the year 1947 a Bedouin youth named Muhammed Adh-Dhib, looking for a lost goat, peered in one of the caves and discovered what the world now knows as the Dead Sea Scrolls.

14

The Riddle of Ephesus

SUDDENLY clamant words rang along the lines of Christendom, like the notes of a bugle, challenging, mysterious, evocative:

John, to the seven churches which are in Asia: Grace be unto you and peace, from him which is and which was and which is to come; and from the seven Spirits which are before his throne . . . I, John, who also am your brother and companion in tribulation, and in the kingdom and patience of Jesus Christ, was in the isle that is called Patmos, for the word of God and for the testimony of Jesus Christ. I was in the Spirit on the Lord's day and heard behind me a great voice, as of a trumpet, saying "I am Alpha and Omega, the first and the last. . . ."

The astonishing book which we know as the Revelation of St John the Divine came from Asia. As the writer tells, it was inspired when he was in Patmos, a small rocky island in the Aegean Sea about sixty miles from Ephesus. Who was the author? Why was he in Patmos? When did he write and what was his aim? Libraries are stacked with books in which these questions are tackled, but mystery broods upon it all, and it is only possible to speculate. One acceptable theory that emerges from the many efforts to interpret the meaning of the work is that much of its magnificent diatribe is directed against Nero. He is the "beast," marked with the number of his name, the slaughterer of the saints; and those who hold the theory say that the author was one stirred to vehement anger by Nero's great persecution of A.D. 64 and its lingering sequences.

A widespread fear haunted men's minds about Nero. His death, though a historic fact, was regarded by Christians as the death of the Antichrist—a creature endowed with supernatural power—and it was felt that he would return to pursue his devil's work. False 'Neros' sprang up, especially in the East, and rumour concerning his resurrection was easily believed by people who hourly looked for the return of their Saviour to rescue them from a Satanic doom. The spirit of Revelation matches the mood of that period. Though most authorities, affected to an extent by a tradition that John was exiled to Patmos by the Emperor Domitian, date the work around A.D. 90–100, a substantial body of opinion prefers to put it twenty or thirty years earlier. That is the view accepted here. Domitian was a persecutor, but not in the massive sense: his attacks were sporadic and limited, and no evidence can be produced that he ever indulged in wholesale massacre such as that to which Revelation refers. The book was widely known to the primitive Church, and may well have been in existence about A.D. 70, when its symbolic affiliations to Nero would have the utmost force and when hatred for his recent enormities would be most likely to inspire it. A generation later the feeling expressed in its pages would hardly have remained at such a burning level.

The opening passages of Revelation indicate that the writer was either one holding high authority among the churches— a kind of archbishop—or one pretending to such authority. The seven churches addressed are those at Ephesus, Smyrna, Pergamos, Thyatira, Sardis, Philadelphia, and Laodicea, and in every case a shrewd knowledge is betrayed of what is going on in each community. Each is called on to hold fast to the true faith and to eschew its particular vices. An otherwise unknown martyr named Antipas is spoken of at Pergamos, and the Thyatirans are rebuked "because thou sufferest that woman Jezebel, which calleth herself a prophetess, to preach."

In contemplating this extraordinary book the whole problem of John, the son of Zebedee, the Beloved Disciple, has to be considered. The traditions are strong and insistent that, after the break-up of the Twelve at Jerusalem, John went sooner or later to live at Ephesus, and eventually died there.

Ephesus was the greatest city in Asia Minor, lifting columned roads to her palatial houses on several hills about the cobalt sea. Her jungle of rickety slums was lost in the lower shadows. The streets were constantly dense with a multi-racial crowd of travellers, vendors, and idlers—Asians of every country, Greeks, Syrians, and Jews, speaking many tongues. It was a noisy, odoriferous city, its unstable population prone to riot and cruelty. It was hot beyond tolerance when the sky turned brassy. Prominent on high rose the vast open-air theatre which could accommodate 30,000 persons, and among its other glittering treasures was one of the wonders of the world—the immense Temple of Diana. It stood beside the harbour, quiet waves breaking at its base, a work of beauty entrancing to the beholder. It was 425 feet long, 220 feet wide, and its 127 Ionic columns— built of Parian marble and each the gift of a king—were 60 feet high. It was not very much shorter and certainly much broader than Canterbury Cathedral. In the heart of the cedar-timbered temple, hidden behind a rich curtain, was the shrine of the goddess—Diana of the Ephesians. The lady was pretty closely related to Aphrodite and Astarte, whose devotees were not distinguished for their morality. Obscene rites were practised around Astarte in particular, and young men qualified as her neophytes by castrating themselves and adopting feminine habits.

From all the world came merchandise to Ephesus, by sea to her famous harbour, and overland, by camel- and mule-train, along the Eastern highways. And from all the world came travellers to gaze on the glory of Diana's temple. In the narrow streets there was a considerable trade in the making of miniature shrines and mementoes of the goddess—a trade carried on by silversmiths, coppersmiths, and craftsmen in many materials. Even terra-cotta and marble were used. Ephesus did good business out of Diana, and the Ephesians were jealous of her repute. Yet here, fifteen years earlier and in spite of such powerful competition, Paul had established a Christian church which, next to that of Antioch, in Syria, had grown to be the most important in the East.

In view of early testimony it is difficult not to believe that here, in this teeming city, John, the Galilean disciple, lived and worked, perhaps when he grew old in some gardened house attached to the meeting-place. Irenaeus, the great Christian writer who was Bishop of Lyons in the second century and whose links with the Apostolic Fathers were strong, makes frequent reference to John, declaring that he was the teacher of Polycarp (whom Irenaeus knew) and that he wrote the Gospel according to St John. Polycarp himself, when Bishop of Smyrna, in about A.D. 150 refused to depart from the Easter observance which he said he had learnt "from John, the disciple of the Lord, and the rest of the Apostles." Polycrates, Bishop of Ephesus, who in about A.D. 190 asserted that he had been a Christian for sixty-five years, wrote: "John, who was both a martyr and a teacher, who reclined on the bosom of the Lord and, being a priest, wore the sacerdotal plate, fell asleep at Ephesus." Tertullian and Clement of Alexandria (about A.D. 180) refer to John in Asia. Clement, describing him as "the Apostle," says he lived at Ephesus.

, Yet confusion arises from what has come down to us of the writing of Papias, Bishop of Hierapolis—a city some hundred miles from Ephesus—in the period between A.D. 100 and A.D. 130. "On any occasion," he declared, "when a person came in my way who had been a follower of the Elders I would inquire about the discourse of the Elders—what Andrew, or Peter, or Philip, or Thomas, or James, or John, or Matthew or any of the Lord's disciples said, and what Aristion and the Elder John, the disciples of the Lord, say."

From this comment has stemmed the belief that there must have been two Johns—the Apostle himself and another described as the Elder; for Papias made it clear that he only had report of John the Apostle at second hand (presumably because he was dead), while he speaks of the Elder John in the present tense, as one who had been living at some period during his own lifetime.

There are reasons for believing that this is the case, that the two men have been mingled in early writings, and that the resultant puzzle offers varied solutions. But there is nothing in this solitary passage of Papias to justify the assumption made by some critics that all references to John at Ephesus must relate only to the one known as the Elder John, and that the traditions concerning John the Apostle must in consequence be set aside. If the cumulative evidence means anything it means that there was, in addition to the Apostle, this other and younger John, also an important Church figure, living simultaneously over many years and then, after the older man's death, into a later period. To accept such a solution is to simplify part of the riddle. For example, Irenaeus asserts that John the Apostle lived until the time of the Emperor Trajan, who assumed the purple in A.D. 98. Any near contemporary of Jesus Christ who lived until A.D. 98 would be aged close on a hundred years, a possible but improbable thing. Yet, conceding that in this particular Irenaeus confused John the Apostle with the Elder John, who was perhaps ten or twelve years younger, we are left with the not unreasonable fact that *he* lived to the age of about eighty-two.

To go into all the details of the Ephesian tangle is a bewildering and fruitless exercise. Every conceivable argument has been elaborated by scholarly commentators. The record of Irenaeus, however much it may stumble in odd particulars, leaves little doubt that his master Polycarp had some early link with John the Apostle. It seems that Polycarp must also have known the Elder John, and that some confusion arises from incidents wrongly attributed to one or other of these men.

In defining the Elder John as a "disciple of the Lord" Papias confirms that he, as well as the Apostle, must have known Jesus in the flesh. This is an important point. It establishes the great authority of the Elder and makes it possible to advance this speculation : that the man known as the Elder John had been a youth of, say, fifteen in the company that followed Jesus, and that later he attached himself to the Apostle John, the Beloved Disciple, and helped him in his missionary work at Ephesus, outliving him probably by more than a decade. Many things fall into a reasonable perspective on such a hypothesis.

Three different writings in the New Testament are attributed to "John"—the Fourth Gospel, three short Epistles, and Revelation. Few dispute that the Gospel and the Epistles were written by the same hand; the manner, argument, and language seem to make it certain, though there are criticisms that the last two

Epistles differ. Yet between these and Revelation there is a world of difference, so that it can be affirmed with some confidence that whoever wrote Revelation did not write the other works. The author of the Fourth Gospel and the Epistles is a tender, persuasive, studious being whose theme is constant— that God is love and that to love one another is the supreme duty. On the other hand, the author of Revelation is a volatile, imaginative man of great virility, quick to anger and terrible in condemnation. His mind ranges heaven and is not afraid of hell. He is all flame and zeal; there is nothing of the pastoral shepherd about him.

If John the Apostle, the son of Zebedee, wrote any of these works, then it would seem to have been Revelation. For his temperament is known to us. Jesus called him one of the "sons of thunder" (an alternative translation is "sons of anger"), and there are two incidents recorded in the Gospels which emphasize his vivid, indignant nature. "Master," he cried at one time, "we saw one casting out devils in thy name, and we forbade him because he followeth not with us." For this impetuosity he got a rebuke, as he did on the next occasion when the inhabitants of a Samaritan village showed discourtesy to Jesus. "Lord, wilt thou that we command fire to come down from heaven and consume them, even as Elias did?" demanded the furious John. "Fire from heaven" is the language of Revelation; it is not the language of the Fourth Gospel or the Epistles.

In the ancient traditions attributed commonly to "John" at Ephesus it is possible to select some typical of each of these men, for they reveal their different characteristics. Irenaeus has a story that one day John, "the disciple of the Lord," went into the baths at Ephesus, but "rushed away from the baths without bathing, and said 'Let us fly lest the baths fall, for Cerinthus, the foe of truth, is inside!'" Cerinthus was a notable heretic. The episode rings true of the son of Zebedee; it is a gesture of violent anger and repudiation. It recalls the same mind that had said, "We forbade him because he followeth not with us." Another story, told in the apocryphal *Acts of John* which dates from about the year A.D. 150, presents us with a personality much more akin to that of the Elder John, and it is so casual, so unimportant, that it has the mark of basic authenticity.

"The blessed evangelist John" was one day stroking a partridge with his hands. A hunter came along. "Aren't you the famous John?" asked the hunter. "What a trivial way for a man like you to be amusing himself."

To this John replied, "What are you carrying?"

"A bow," answered the hunter.

"Then why don't you always carry it stretched?" asked John. The hunter explained that if the bow were constantly stretched taut its vitality would be exhausted and it would grow soft.

"Quite right, young man," answered John. "And that is why this brief relaxation of my mind should not puzzle you. For unless it relaxes sometimes and eases itself it will become slack through perpetual application."

Here is a glimpse of some one who is certainly no "son of thunder," but one much more like the writer of the Epistles and the Fourth Gospel—a man distinguished for gentleness, whose mind was tranquil, who had a smile for the hunter and an affectionate hand for the partridge. A further picture from primitive times more strikingly identifies the author of these books. It describes how, when "John" was an old man, he had to be carried about and was constantly blessing those around him with the words, "Little children, love one another." Consider this in the light of phrases in the First Epistle of John: "My little children, these things I write unto you. . . . I write unto you, little children, because your sins are forgiven you. . . . Little children, it is the last time."

This fatherly, pastoral voice is in utter contrast to the vehemence of the Apostle, who seems to have been a typically passionate and reckless Galilean. Peter shared some of the same qualities; he was impulsive and emotional. It is interesting that these two fervent men were admitted, beyond the rest of the Twelve, to the intimacy of Jesus. The one, John the Beloved Disciple, "lay on his breast"—an expression which probably means that he shared his Master's couch at supper. To the other were given the keys of the Kingdom.

Though all these clues and hints are patchy and far-off, they make it possible to hazard the speculation that John the Apostle, the son of Zebedee, lived until somewhere around A.D. 85, dying where he had long dwelt, at Ephesus. In view of the indulgent affection Jesus had for him he may well have been a rather younger man, perhaps only in his middle twenties at the time of the Crucifixion. His protégé and companion was the one described as the Elder John, who in early youth had also known Jesus. The Apostle during his lifetime had supervised the work of the various churches in Asia, and he might have been the author—in part, at least—of Revelation. On his death the care of the Asian churches fell to his intimate, the Elder John, who wrote the Epistles and also the Gospel according to St John. Into that Gospel he put those things he had been told by his old master, but he fashioned it according to his own more scholarly and interpretive ways and in the light of his own information. Both the men whose minds and recollections went to its making had known Jesus, even though one of them had only been a boy; hence, "we beheld his glory, the glory of the only begotten of the Father, full of grace and truth." May it not also explain the closing words of the Gospel, where, referring to "the disciple whom Jesus loved," the writer comments, "This is the disciple which testifieth of these things and wrote these things; and we know that his testimony is true." The possibility that the Apostle John had bequeathed written matter which was used by the compiler of the Gospel is here evident.

The Gospel of John bears some evidence that its author was acquainted with the Gospel of Mark, which would be reasonable enough. But it contains much narrative, particularly relating to the trial and Crucifixion, not to be found elsewhere. It sparkles with touches that reveal personal knowledge. For example, describing how the High Priest's servant was attacked when he came to arrest Jesus, the narrator adds, "The servant's name was Malchus." Again, Pilate's judgment seat, not located in the other Gospels, is by John set "in a place that is called the Pavement." Excavation in Jerusalem during the present century has established the existence of a fine Roman pavement in the very position where, as a seat of judgment, it might have been expected—where the Tower of Antonia, the Imperial headquarters, used to stand. Visitors to-day to another Roman garrison city—York—may walk along what still bears its ancient name—Pavement.

It is admittedly difficult to believe that Revelation was written by John the Apostle, and the argument that it was composed by somebody else, around A.D. 95–100, following Domitian's cruel reign, has become almost accepted as fact. But scepticism about antique origins is not infrequently proven to be unmerited, and it needs to be borne in mind that some of the most illustrious scholars have held to the earlier date. Interpretations of the mystic number 666 (or 616) can be made to fit almost any theory and lead nowhere. The whole riddle is not only baffling but is made more complex by the literature to which it has given rise. Nobody has been able to prove that John had nothing to do with Revelation. He could have had.

Moreover, there is a tradition that John visited Rome and was tormented with boiling oil during one of the persecutions. The rumour is thin, but it has some vague association with the oil-soaked "tunics of pain" to which history bears witness. It is conceivable that after some maltreatment the Apostle returned to the East, staying awhile in the quietude of Patmos before resuming his heavy task at Ephesus. There, burning with anger and distress at all the horrors he had seen in Rome, he was inspired to project the mighty book of denunciation and prophecy, with its arraignment of Neronic imperialism:

> And I stood upon the sand of the sea, and saw a beast rise up out of the sea, having seven heads and ten horns, and upon his horns ten crowns, and upon his heads the name of blasphemy. . . . Let him that hath understanding count the number of the beast: for it is the number of a man; and his number is six hundred threescore and six.

And its fanatical execration of Rome:

> And I saw a woman sit upon a scarlet coloured beast, full of names of blasphemy, having seven heads and ten horns. And the woman was arrayed in purple and scarlet colour, and decked with gold and precious stones and pearls, having a golden cup in her hand full of abominations and filthiness of her fornication; and upon her forehead was a name written MYSTERY, BABYLON

THE GREAT, THE MOTHER OF HARLOTS AND ABOMINATIONS OF THE EARTH. And I saw the woman drunken with the blood of the saints and with the blood of the martyrs of Jesus.

Is there no frenzied recollection here mingled with this symbolism—no reeking immortality for Poppaea Sabina in these lines?

15

The Herodian Woman

TURNING off the main coast road of Israel that crosses the verdant plain of Sharon, you follow a track towards the sea: it is a lumpy track, for the red earth has been pounded by tractors and carts. Wild mimosa hangs in springtime in cataracts of gold along the verge, and there are neat vineyards and groves of late oranges that tip the warm air with piercing fragrance. You come to a gate and a tangle of wire where the soil begins to merge into sand-dunes. A few hundred yards away Mediterranean rollers crash on the shore, throwing up white spume that flashes like an intermittent curtain between your eyes and the deep blue of the distance. Passing through the gate, you reach an excavation—a quadrangle cut out of the earth. There are walls, massive broken columns, foliated capitals, a pavement with a Greek inscription, and, towering like the dumb witness of Ozymandias, two gigantic headless statues.

They are seated figures, carved in the classic Roman manner —sandalled dignitaries, the very folds of whose robes imply a serene eminence and evoke an instant comprehension of the pomp and circumstance amid which they were first erected. Each ends at a muscular neck from which, as if to mock the inquirer, time has wrested the face that might have afforded recognition. You stare up at them in wonderment while only the music of the breaking sea disturbs the prevailing silence. Whose were the proud heads that once crowned them? The question goes unanswered, but there they sit, unknown and for ever mysterious, testifying to a whole race of Emperors and stern procurators who, from this spot, exerted power over Judaea. For these statues and walls, and a few stones beside the sea, are all that now mark Caesarea, the seat of Imperial

I

administration; all that identify the magnificent city where
Pontius Pilate and Paul, and Philip the Evangelist and Luke,
and Felix and the lovely Drusilla and Agrippa and Berenice
played incidents in the great Christian drama.

After the fall of Jerusalem it was necessarily here to Caesarea
that Titus came, to secure his prisoners, arrange the new
administration, and decide the dispersal of his forces. But he
did not stay long, for a woman's arms were waiting for him at
that other Caesarea—Caesarea Philippi, in the north—and he
hastened to them with the impetuosity of a man willingly
enslaved. They were the arms of Berenice.

Agrippa, though nominally the King of the Jews, had un-
waveringly supported the Roman cause. It may be said in his
defence that he endeavoured from the first to prevent his people
from taking up arms against Caesar, arguing rightly that they
would be crushed. Both he and his sister had tried reason—she
even with the despicable Florus—but reason had failed. They
chose the winning side—a Herodian habit not lightly to be condemned if diplomacy in a cynical world has any virtue. Between
Agrippa and Titus a close friendship sprang up; between Titus
and Berenice a passionate love-affair developed. They had lived
together at different times during the campaign in Palestine,
and now that fighting had ended the Roman prince was determined to relax in her company and enjoy the praises and kisses
of her not inexperienced lips.

Her brother prepared a lavish entertainment for the conqueror at Caesarea Philippi, conveniently ignoring the utter
devastation that had been wrought in the ancient home of his
race. Agrippa was not one who could cry, "If I forget thee, O
Jerusalem, let my right hand forget her cunning." He retained
the cunning and forgot the city.

Berenice, born in the year before the Crucifixion, was now
aged forty-two—nine years older than Titus—but her fascination bound him to her utterly. It is impossible to survey her life
without a feeling of compassion, for she early suffered the barb
of Juvenal, the cold contempt of Tacitus, and even the dislike
of that adroit trimmer Josephus; and, of course, the unco guid
have long consigned her to hell. At about sixteen she was

married to her uncle, Herod of Chalcis, bearing him two sons. On his death she began an incestuous liaison with her brother, but when the scandal became public she left him and married King Poleman of Cilicia, who underwent circumcision in order to gain her. This marriage did not last long, and she returned to her brother's bed, a state of affairs that continued until, in Titus, she found the man of her desires. Such a record cannot be accommodated either by morality or ethics, but Berenice seems to have been one of those highly sexed, intense, and clever women who are to be found in all ages, haunted by a fever for erotic fufilment that leads them into courses from which, while offending the social code, they derive little contentment for themselves.

That she was beautiful and desirable there can be no doubt, yet even with these assets she was dissatisfied, for she was not so lovely as her younger sister Drusilla, and in earlier years had tormented the child jealously. She had phases of religious enthusiasm when she undertook stern Jewish penances—a form of emotional outlet typical of such women. The nymphomaniac is prone, if not to prayer, at least to ritual. She must have been eager and of quick intelligence to win the devotion of Titus, for he had keen discrimination and culture.

Though a commander of great brilliance and bravery, Titus was in no sense a rough, homespun soldier. Physically he was not really robust, nor were his handsome features of the 'tough' variety. His manners were winning rather than assertive, and the people of Rome adored him even if he could be cruel. He was fond of music and poetry, and took a laughing pride in being able to write shorthand more efficiently than his secretaries. A lustful woman may well have appealed to a man of this temperament, for sexual comprehension is more developed in such men than in the hearty, athletic type; but she could not have held his devotion, as Berenice did for years, had she lacked qualities of mind and presence amid which he could exercise, and find delight for, his own.

Weeks of feasting, entertainment, and embracing now followed at Caesarea Philippi, Agrippa pouring out his well-stored coffers in honour of the heir to the Empire, his friend and his sister's lover. Exciting shows were presented in the amphi-theatre. Jewish prisoners were compelled to fight with wild beasts and gladiators. There was an appropriate prodigality of blood as well as of food and wine. When, in October, it was time to move on the jubilations continued at Antioch, and then down in Egypt, before Titus set sail for Rome. It would seem that throughout this triumphal tour Berenice continued to live with the conqueror; they were probably the happiest months of both their lives.

No Roman triumph exceeded in splendour and excitement that which Titus shared with his father, Vespasian, in the early summer of A.D. 71. Although the Senate had decreed that each should be honoured with a separate celebration, the Emperor preferred to have a joint one only. The capital poured its multi-tude into the streets, the procession wound its magnificent way past the Forum, and all the treasures of conquest were displayed so that none could doubt the utter destruction of the Jews. Soldiers, horse and foot, marched jubilantly, escorting their loot, including the massive *menorah*, or branched candlestick, from the Temple, and the gold and silver they had ravished there. Seven hundred Jewish prisoners carried their chains through the derisively howling mob. Flowers and oak-leaves were strewn in the path of Vespasian and Titus. At the traditional point the procession halted while the brave Simon Bar Giora, who had resisted Rome to the end, was dragged away to be strangled. The crowd yelled its garlicked joy, the cymbals clashed, and the glory went on. But before the day ended the Emperor grew bored and slightly disgusted; he went home to bed and his mis-tresses, leaving Titus to hold the final receptions.

Thus Rome celebrated the destitution of Jerusalem and that dispersal of the Jewish people which was to continue for nearly two thousand years, until, in our own time, they were able to stand again on Zion. It was hardly possible for the Christians in Rome to participate in the festal occasion even had they desired to do so. The prejudice then existing would make it a matter of satisfaction to them that the Jewish power had been broken, for they conceived the Jews to have been solely responsible for the death of Christ. Yet, by an irony of fate, they were themselves looked upon still as a sect associated with Judaism, and discretion would keep them to their houses. Nevertheless, the destruction of Jerusalem and the Temple must have been a momentous event in the minds of Bishop Linus and his immediate associates, Clement and Anencletus. Whether they realized it or not, it meant that Rome, and not Jerusalem, was destined to be the centre of their faith and that the Judaic interpretation of Christianity was doomed. True, the constant souls in Pella, still led by Simeon, the cousin of Jesus, were to continue for a while, venerated as the lineal descendants of the original Nazarenes, but their weakened authority now had a term to it, and the Church was to flourish under the Pauline rather than the Jacobean influence.

Yet Rome itself, though consecrated by the martyrdom of Peter and Paul, had not yet the pre-eminence over Asia, for it was in Asia that the surviving disciples, so far as they are traceable, continued to work—John the Apostle, Andrew the Apostle, Philip the Evangelist, and the Elder John. They were gathered in the neighbourhood of Ephesus, and it is reasonable to believe that they visited the churches of Smyrna, Pergamos, and other Asian cities, probably on occasion going as far as Antioch, where the Christian cause continued to flourish and echoes of Peter and Paul still reverberated.

During this decade—A.D. 70 to A.D. 80—Luke, the physician and faithful travelling companion of Paul, wrote his Gospel. It was addressed to one Theophilus, about whom nothing is known, and it was, of course, followed by the Acts of the Apostles, written by the same hand. Luke is reported to have lived to the age of seventy and to have died in Bithynia, but whether he retired to that distant province in order to put down his record of events or whether, in the first instance, he went back to Antioch, his native city, during the reign of Vespasian is a matter for fruitless debate. None can say. Luke was a literary man, the most accomplished writer of them all. He had not been himself a witness of the events described in the Gospel, and the scholarly manner in which he approached the task presupposes careful research. In the course of that research he may well have consulted surviving disciples, and for that pur-

pose a residence in Antioch would have been convenient. His
introduction implies all this and a determination to be both
painstaking and accurate:

> Forasmuch as many have taken in hand to set forth, in order,
> a declaration of those things which are most surely believed
> among us, even as they delivered them unto us which from the
> beginning were eyewitnesses and ministers of the Word; it
> seemed good to me also, having had perfect understanding of all
> things from the very first, to write unto thee in order, most
> excellent Theophilus, that thou mightest know the certainty of
> those things wherein thou hast been instructed.

But these affairs were in greatest measure unknown to the
rulers of Rome, or regarded as of little moment. How rarely do
men recognize their conquerors until it is too late! Vespasian,
justly conscious that he had served the State well, now took life
easily, delegating more and more responsibility to Titus. He
acquiesced in some decisions following the Jewish rebellion, one
of which was that all claimants to membership of the royal
house of David should be rooted out. They were regarded as a
source of dangerous trouble, much as the house of Stuart was
regarded in England after the Forty-five. The Emperor took a
keen interest in the building of a huge new amphitheatre—
that which is known as the Colosseum, whose gaunt walls still
stand in Rome. It was destined to be a morbid memorial of the
Flavian dynasty and the scene of more blood-letting and sadistic
entertainment than any of its grim predecessors, for even Nero
was outdone in massacre of man and beast by the Colosseum
management during the next few decades.

Titus was the light of his father's eyes as he was the joy of
the Roman people. The ageing Emperor cared little that his
eldest son had brought Berenice, the Jewish princess, to live
with him at the palace. The lad was entitled to his love-life, and
the woman was beautiful and of noble birth: this was less dis-
turbing and expensive than a string of hussies might have
been. But Vespasian's younger son, the brooding, suspicious,
red-headed Domitian, was probably among those who professed
other views to the Roman aristocracy, and there was murmuring against the liaison, which grew deeper as the years passed.

Nevertheless, Berenice seems to have held her station in Rome as wife in all but legal sanction of the heir to the throne, and she received the honour due to his consort. Perhaps during this proud period she enjoyed being able to patronize her sister Drusilla and her husband Felix, the former procurator of Judaea, if they were still living at Rome. Nor is it far-fetched to assume that a present was dispatched from the palace on the occasion of the marriage of Drusilla's son, the little boy who had run about the *praetorium* at Caesarea in the days when Paul was a captive there. For the wedding must have taken place towards the end of this decade.

Vespasian never lost his affection for his native village and its onion soup. No power, and no diversionary pomp, shook the old man's steadfast loyalty to the things he savoured best. And it was there at Reate, amid the fields of his childhood, that fatal illness seized him in A.D. 79. To the end he kept his stout heart and sense of fitness. Shortly before he died he tried to struggle out of bed, saying, "An Emperor should die standing." His parting words, muttered, we may believe, with a last brave twinkle in his eye, were: "I have an idea I'm about to become a god." He had always seen through the nonsense by which dead Emperors were deified.

Exactly fifty years had gone by since the crucifixion of Jesus Christ when Vespasian died and Titus became Emperor.

The ancient historians affirm that, on his succession, Titus dismissed Berenice because of public disfavour. The implication is that the people, while turning a blind eye on a young prince's peccadillo, were not ready to tolerate like conduct in a reigning monarch. She was, of course, a Jewess, and that cannot have endeared her to Roman citizens; but the popularity of Titus was such that a great deal of leniency would have been extended to him. If he was faced with the cruel choice, the Empire or his love, there is nothing to suggest that it was forced on him by popular agitation. A more likely interpretation is that some kind of palace clique brought pressure to bear. Domitian could have been active in any manoeuvre calculated to embarrass Titus, for that unlikable character seems to have harboured envy and jealousy in full measure.

Whatever the detailed influences may have been, the decision is beyond doubt. Berenice quit the Capitol, left Rome, and returned to Palestine, presumably to the shelter of her brother's roof. There she disappears from all record, either to embark on some unknown phase of a vicious and vagarious career, or to pass her later years in remorseful indifference. Too little is known about the whole transaction to apportion blame or praise. Titus had passed the most vivid peak of his life, and what little remained to him was shadowed by anxiety and loneliness, even though his brow was now laurelled with the supreme power. His people called him "the darling of the human race"; fate was not so fond. Within a few weeks of his accession an appalling natural calamity fell upon Italy, and this was followed some months later by another serious fire in Rome and a pestilence that caused heavy loss of life.

At this period one of the most promising young Romans was Gaius Plinius Caecilius Secundus, known to posterity as Pliny the Younger. He was now in his nineteenth year, finishing his studies and about to appear as a brilliant advocate. He little knew that his chief claim to fame would rest on certain dealings he was to have with the despised Christian sect. During the summer of A.D. 79 he stayed on the Bay of Naples with his uncle, Pliny the Elder, who, as scientific writer and administrator, was celebrated throughout the Empire. This elder Pliny was now Prefect of the Fleet at Misenum, and he had a house in the neighbourhood.

On August 24, at about one o'clock in the afternoon, young Pliny's mother called the older man's attention to an extraordinary cloud. He roused himself from sun-bathing, slipped on his shoes, and climbed a near-by knoll, where a better view could be obtained. The cloud rose to an enormous height above the peak of Vesuvius: it was shaped like a pine-tree with rapidly spreading branches; its colour changed from white to black as intermittent deluges of rock and cinders were flung up within it. For the moment nobody seemed to understand that disaster was overwhelming the inhabitants of Pompeii and Herculaneum, at the foot of the volcano. The elder Pliny, his scientific interest excited by the cloud phenomenon, ordered a swift boat to be got ready and asked his nephew if he would care to accompany him on a trip across the bay to see what it was all about. Pliny junior replied that he preferred to study, his uncle having given him an essay to write. By this decision he may well have saved his life.

As the older man left the house to hasten to the boat a message arrived from Rectina, the wife of one Bassus, who had a villa near Pompeii. She begged immediate assistance, as the only possible escape was by sea. Instantly the Prefect of the Fleet, realizing what was occurring, gave orders for war-galleys to be launched to the rescue of the threatened people, himself directing his light bark straight for the belching mountain.

Cataracts of burning ash, scorched boulders, and pumice crashed upon the ships as they drew near the stricken coast. Then the sea, recoiling from the splintered earth, ebbed in a steaming tide. Landslides thundered down to the shore, blocking hope of approach. Although it was still day, ebony darkness had descended, illumined only by broad sheets of flame that leapt skyward from the molten cone of Vesuvius. Pliny insisted on getting somehow to land, and found his way to the home of a friend named Pomponianus, where he tried to reassure the terrified household. Then, amid all this horror, the extraordinary man went to bed, his after-luncheon rest having been so rudely interrupted. But when the courtyard became so deep in ash and lava that his escape was threatened they aroused him.

Should they stay indoors or wander about in the open? The question became vehemently pressing, for the whole house now began to shudder and sway backward and forward. They all went out, fastening pillows and towels over their heads to protect themselves from the showers of hot cinders. They decided to make for the shore in the hope of getting to safety by sea, but when they came there the waves were tempestuous and subject to perilous tides, making all attempt hopeless. Pliny lay down on a piece of discarded sail-cloth on the beach; he asked for a drink of water. He was a fat man, and his exertions were proving too much.

Suddenly assaulted by driving flame and sulphurous smoke, those around him fled, and Pliny himself tried to rise, but collapsed. Three days later, when pallid light at last returned to the devastated region, his body was found, unbruised.

These details were given afterwards in a letter from Pliny the Younger to his friend Cornelius Tacitus, the famous historian. Only a year earlier Tacitus had married the daughter of Julius Agricola, who at this time, as Governor of Britain, was engaged in bitter fighting with the warrior tribes of northern England and Scotland.

The Roman world was stunned by the terrible eruption of Vesuvius; thousands had died and immense damage was done. Titus poured out his personal fortune to relieve the consequent distress, and many of the injured and homeless were cared for under his immediate protection. But among those who were past human aid were Agrippa, the young son of Drusilla, and his bride; they died in one of the buried towns where they had gone for the summer months. Thus the child of Caesarea did not long outlive the great Apostle who had once appeared before his father's judgment seat.

Nor had time much more to offer the beloved Emperor. In the late summer of A.D. 81 he was taken ill with the prevailing fever when staying at the family home at Reate, where his father had died. As he lay sick and exhausted he had a premonition that he would not recover. He looked up to the sunny sky and protested that he did not really deserve to die, "for there was only one fact in his life of which he had need to repent." Sage historians, puzzled by this enigmatic remark, have vainly searched the fragmentary records to discover what act of civil policy or military impulse he could have been referring to. They seem to have forgotten Berenice. Did Titus regret the association, or was he ashamed that he had cast her off? The secret died with him in his forty-second year.

Yet another had passed away during this fever-haunted period —Linus, Bishop of Rome and immediate successor of Peter. The elders chose Anencletus to take his place, a man about whom nothing is known apart from his name. It was a name sometimes borne by slaves (as an inscription found in London helps to testify), and suggests that, like Clement who was to succeed him, the new bishop was a freedman of lowly parentage.

16

The Dark Domitian

DOMITIAN was only twenty-nine when he became
Emperor. Those who had been close to him in youth
cannot have been deceived by the appearance of tolera-
tion and restraint with which he invested the beginning of his
rule. His was an involved and to some extent contradictory
character—secretive and introspective, yet given to reckless
action. In that mysterious way by which public opinion forms
sound judgment concerning remote and powerful personages, the
Roman people felt uneasy about their new sovereign from the
moment he was bedecked with the purple. He came in like an
east wind and froze the geniality that Titus had exhaled. He had
a certain ability, but there was no milk of human kindness
within him. It is possible that the glowing merits of his elder
brother had been so obviously preferred by their father, Vespasian, as they were adored and praised by the common people,
that he nursed the general grievances of such as are made to
feel inferior. This could account for the jealousy and suspicion
that were his dominant traits. A report that he had poisoned
Titus gained currency; it was doubtless untrue, but it reflected
the mistrust with which he was regarded. Men felt with much
justification that the Flavian line, at its inception so refreshing
and sane after its lunatic predecessors, might well grow into a
semblance of those dangerous degenerates.

Yet outwardly Domitian began well. He professed concern for
the State religions, built new temples, and applied himself personally to the administration of justice. Towards Vespasian's
distinguished nephew, his own cousin Flavius Clemens, he
showed marked favour, advancing him to high office. Clemens
was married to Domitilla, Domitian's niece, and the Emperor

conferred the names of Vespasian and Domitian on their two
young sons, announcing that they were to be his successors in
due course. These developments, however much they may have
been tinctured with doubt, must have given some hope to the
Christians in Rome, for Flavius Clemens' household was a
Christian one, and the prospect of a member of the faith
becoming Emperor at no distant date held out glittering possi-
bilities for the cause throughout the civilized world. When,
probably around the year A.D. 88, Anencletus died and Clement
became Bishop of Rome there would be the closest contact
between him and this branch of the Imperial family if Dr
Lightfoot's theory is accepted that he was, in fact, one of Flavius
Clemens' freedmen. The theory may be criticized as something
of an enlightened guess, yet the strands of fact and date, as
they present themselves, certainly make it tenable.

But during this period Domitian cast away camouflage and
revealed himself in all his cold and cruel meanness. The open
change occurred after a revolt among the legions of Upper
Germany. This revolt was speedily crushed, but it unleased the
full range of the Emperor's dark and miscreant mind. He
trusted nobody, and those who were nearest to him were the
particular objects of his malevolence. Friends and Ministers
alike were hurled from office, banished, or put to death. He
raked the very ashes of the fire to discover treacherous elements.
Conceiving that every hand was against him, he went in hourly
fear of assassination. Those who survived his hatred were
regarded afterwards as deserving other men's doubts in consequence. Pliny the Younger was one of these. He held and
retained office under Domitian, as overseer of the military
accounts, while one of the ablest and most honourable servants
of the State suffered humiliating dismissal. This was Agricola,
Governor of Britain, who, because he was brilliantly victorious
and successful, drew on himself the Emperor's venomous
jealousy. He was recalled and sent into compulsory retirement.

Domitian applied the strictest supervision to his provincial
governors, and, as at home so abroad, the probe of his mis-
trustful brain was felt. He was frightened of rebellion. Decrees
that had grown stagnant through neglect were stirred afresh.

including that by which descendants of the Jewish royal house were to be sought out. The pursuit of this order brought forward two suspects who, according to Hegesippus, were interrogated by the Emperor himself. This may be attributed to figurative language. It is much more probable that they appeared in front of an officer acting under the Imperial legate in Syria, for they were hardly important enough to be sent to Rome at the public expense.

They were two young men who freely acknowledged that they were grandsons of Jude, the stepbrother of Jesus the Messiah, and were, therefore, of the line of David. Their clothes were poor, their speech was simple and provincial, and their questioner felt pity mingled with contempt for their abysmal fall from regal status. When he asked them about their means they said they had between them some £35. They showed him their hands, toil-torn and calloused, explaining that they depended for their livelihood on the produce of a smallholding about twenty acres in extent. They emphasized that they had no interest in political issues, or indeed in temporal affairs generally, for they rested all their expectations on the life to come. They were dismissed as harmless peasants, incapable of conspiring against the Empire.

These two grandsons of Jude are the last representatives of the family from Nazareth—save Simeon, then in Pella—of whom history has any record. In what part of Judaea they tilled their little farm is not certain, though they appear to have referred to a village called "Cocaba." Southward of Lydda, on the fertile coastal plain of Israel, near the road to Beersheba, there is to-day a hamlet bearing the name Kokaba.

In A.D. 95 Flavius Clemens was Consul in Rome, seemingly high and sunlit in the glance of the Emperor, yet the clouds swept down on him immediately his term of office came to an end. Soldiers wheeled into his courtyard, and he and his wife Domitilla were taken into custody on an Imperial warrant accusing them of "atheism" and of "Jewish leanings"—in other words, of being Christians. Suetonius, a contemporary writer, describes Flavius Clemens as *"contemptissimae inertiae"*—contemptibly indolent, a remark implying gross neglect of Roman festivals and customary duties. Christians were often identified by their default in this respect. Refusal to participate in required observances called for high courage, especially from those of social or political eminence. In a memorable passage Gibbon has set forth the acute problems with which they were confronted:

The dangerous temptations which on every side lurked in ambush to surprise the unguarded believer assailed him with redoubled violence on the days of solemn festivals. So artfully were they framed and disposed throughout the year that superstition always wore the appearance of pleasure, and often of virtue. Some of the most sacred festivals in the Roman ritual were destined to salute the new calends of January with vows of public and private felicity; to indulge the pious remembrance of the dead and living; to ascertain the inviolable bounds of property; to hail, on the return of spring, the genial powers of fecundity; to perpetuate the two memorable eras of Rome, the foundation of the city and that of the republic; and to restore, during the humane licence of the Saturnalia, the primitive equality of mankind. Some idea may be conceived of the abhorrence of the Christians for such impious ceremonies by the scrupulous delicacy which they displayed on a much less alarming occasion. On days of general festivity it was the custom of the ancients to adorn their doors with lamps and with branches of laurel, and to crown their heads with a garland of flowers. This innocent and elegant practice might perhaps have been tolerated as a mere civil institution. But it most unluckily happened that the doors were under the protection of the household gods, that the laurel was sacred to the lover of Daphne, and that garlands of flowers, though frequently worn as a symbol either of joy or mourning, had been dedicated in their first origin to the service of superstition. The trembling Christians, who were persuaded in this instance to comply with the fashion of their country and the commands of the magistrate, laboured under the most gloomy apprehensions from the reproaches of their own conscience, the censures of the Church, and the denunciations of divine vengeance. Such was the anxious diligence which was required to guard the chastity of the Gospel from the infectious breath of idolatry. The superstitious observances of public or private rites were carelessly practised, from education and habit, by the followers of the established religion. But as often as they occurred they afforded the Christians an opportunity of declaring and confirming their zealous opposition.

The treatment of Flavius Clemens was typical of Domitian's

methods. His cruelty was depraved and excessive. A victim, on the eve of his destruction, was encouraged to believe that he enjoyed the Emperor's confidence to the full. On the day before issuing an order for his crucifixion he invited one of his stewards to his bedroom, chatted amiably with him, making him sit beside the royal presence on the couch, and sent the poor fellow away exhilarated by such marks of favour. He rarely pronounced sentence of death without giving the condemned man hope of reprieve by dwelling on the virtues of mercy. Towards the close of his reign he was the same creature that he had been in youth, when his favourite pastime was to hunt flies with a specially pointed stiletto.

Flavius Clemens was put to death and his wife Domitilla was exiled for life to the grim island of Pandateria, that abode of sorrow and agony where Octavia, Nero's innocent wife, had been murdered.

Rome in general must have been dismayed by the fall of one so high in the State, but to the Christians it was a truly lamentable event. Bishop Clement suffered a personal bereavement in the loss of his old master and friend. Other "atheists" were also killed by the Emperor's command, and a general persecution seemed imminent. Whether the Christians went underground it is impossible to say, but that they were preoccupied with the peril in which they found themselves emerges plainly from the opening sentences of a famous document which Clement composed shortly afterwards. This was a letter from the Church in Rome to the Church in Corinth, and it begins with these words: "Owing to the sudden and repeated misfortunes and calamities which have befallen us we consider that our attention has been somewhat delayed in turning to the questions disputed among you, beloved . . ."

Fortunate were the Christians of Rome that they had a man like Clement to lead them under these "repeated calamities." He was practical and balanced. His devotion to the Cross sprang not from hysterical fervour, but from deep wells of passion and conviction. His strength lay in reason, understanding, and a profound veneration for the Scriptures. From his personal acquaintance with Peter and Paul and their friends he drew authority. For many years his letter to the Corinthians, despatched probably at the end of A.D. 95 or at the beginning of A.D. 96, was read in churches in many parts of the world as an Epistle having Apostolic significance. It remains a splendid and heroic affirmation of the faith, uttered at a time of distress and to a faltering community. Implicit in it is a sense of that supremacy which the Church in Rome later claimed, but it is marked by compassion, humility, and affection.

The occasion which evoked it was a conflict in the Church in Corinth that had led to the deposition of some presbyters; and it should be borne in mind that, at this time, the individual churches were ruled by executives of presbyters and deacons over which the bishop presided, not so much as an all-influential person, but as a kind of chairman. To eject presbyters by revolt or criticism, other than for gross personal misdemeanour, was to strike at the true Word of the Gospel. By exhortation, advice, and gentle rebuke Clement put forward the orthodox case.

> We are not only writing these things to you, beloved, for your admonition, but also to remind ourselves; for we are in the same arena and the same struggle is before us. Wherefore let us put aside empty and vain cares, and let us come to the glorious and venerable rule of our tradition, and let us see what is good and pleasing and acceptable in the sight of our Maker. . . . For Christ is of those who are humble-minded, not of those who exalt themselves over his flock. . . . Let us consider, beloved, how the Master continually proves to us that there will be a future resurrection, of which he has made the first-fruits by raising the Lord Jesus Christ from the dead. Let us look, beloved, at the resurrection which is taking place at its proper season. Day and night show us a resurrection. The night sleeps, the day arises; the day departs, night comes on. Let us take the crops: how and in what way does the sowing take place? "The sower went forth to sow" and cast each of the seeds into the ground; and they fall on to the ground, parched and bare, and suffer decay; then from their decay the greatness of the providence of the Master raises them up, and from one grain more grow and bring forth fruit.

The doctrine of Apostolic succession is declared:

> The Apostles received the Gospel for us from the Lord Jesus Christ. Jesus the Christ was sent from God. The Christ, therefore, is from God and the Apostles from the Christ. . . . Our Apostles

also knew through our Lord Jesus Christ that there would be strife for the title of bishop. For this cause, therefore, since they had received perfect foreknowledge, they appointed those who have been already mentioned, and afterwards added the codicil that if they should fall asleep other approved men should succeed to their ministry. We consider, therefore, that it is not just to remove from their ministry those who were appointed by them, or later on by other eminent men, with the consent of the whole Church, and have ministered to the flock of Christ without blame, humbly, peaceably and disinterestedly. . . . You, therefore, who laid the foundations of the sedition, submit to the Presbyters and receive the correction of repentance, bending the knees of your hearts. . . . It is better for you to be found small but honourable in the flock of Christ than to be pre-eminent in repute but to be cast out from his hope.

This is a confident, calm voice. A firm but charitable leader is speaking. He ends his 12,000-word epistle with a blessing of great beauty.

Three men were chosen to carry this important letter to Corinth and to act as delegates on behalf of Rome. They were Claudius Ephebus, Valerius Vito, and Fortunatus. Clement describes them to the Corinthians as "faithful and prudent men who have lived among us without blame from youth to old age, and they shall be witnesses between you and us." The term "old age" probably means that they were in their sixties, for an arduous and dangerous mission would hardly have been entrusted to men verging on infirmity; yet the fact that they had been members of the Christian community since their youth suggests that they belonged to the original company under Peter and Paul. During Paul's stay in Rome they would have been in their late twenties or early thirties. But two of them can be even more significantly identified. The royal prefixes, Claudius and Valerius, imply membership of the Imperial service as slaves or freedmen, and it is highly probable that these two were among those Christians "of Caesar's household" from whom Paul had sent greetings in his Epistle to the Philippians. This incident underlines what is prone to be forgotten: that at the close of the first century there were many still actively engaged in gallant work for the Church who had known, and been known by, the Apostles.

K

During a period like this, when the cunning Domitian had his evil eye fixed on "atheists and Judaizers" it was no enviable job to smuggle a document such as Clement's letter across a wide and populous part of the Empire. Quick-thinking, adroit minds were required, to say nothing of stout hearts. Each man probably had a copy. They may have taken different routes through Italy and across the sea to Greece. Friends, and friendly bolt-holes, would be known at various points of call, and among shipmasters and their crews would be Christian agents. It is difficult to imagine how messages were transmitted other than on the assumption that an intricate grape-vine existed; but even so there must have been excitement and adventure in plenty for these carriers of forbidden propaganda as they eluded the Imperial watch. Being a Christian in Domitian's reign had the perils and thrills known to members of the Maquis during the Hitler war. It was not a matter of taking tea at the vicarage.

Nor did meekness and long-suffering monopolize conduct on what might be called the political front. There was a steward of the exiled, and now widowed, Lady Domitilla whose name was Stephanus. It cannot be proven that he was a Christian, but the odds are heavily in favour of his being so, for her household would not be likely to harbour any who opposed the faith. Stephanus meditated revenge for his mistress and probably convinced himself that what he contemplated was in the service of humanity. The less charitable might say it was certainly in his own interest because he had come under suspicion of misappropriating funds. There is no need to manufacture too golden a mainspring for his deed: it is enough that he was brought to the sticking-point.

The Emperor's cruelties had inevitably resulted in a conspiracy against him in which the Empress herself, threatened with untimely death at his untender hands, was involved. But the conspiracy appears to have been very much a hole-and-corner affair until Stephanus joined it and took the lead. He laid his plans with subtlety, and for some days was seen wearing a heavy bandage round his forearm, giving out that he had injured himself. But within the bandage was a knife. Then, trading on the Emperor's suspicious mind, he sent him a message indicating that he wished to unburden himself of details about a revolutionary plot that had been confided to him. On September 18, A.D. 96, Domitian granted him a private interview, satisfied that he could be in no danger from a man with a helpless right arm.

Stephanus, on entering the room bowed and presented a scroll. Assuming that this contained details of the conspiracy and the names of those who formed it, Domitian took the document and turned aside to study its contents. Immediately the steward whipped out the knife from his bandage and plunged it in the Emperor's groin.

What followed was seen by a young boy who stood in attendance on the Emperor and was paralyzed with fear and horror. Domitian was a tall, muscular man, even though he was now fat and bald-headed, He grappled with Stephanus, and both of them crashed to the floor, Stephanus stabbing viciously, the Emperor trying to gouge out his enemy's eyes with his fingernails. As they rolled and gasped in this deadly embrace Domitian shouted for help and called on the boy to give him a dagger that he kept under the coverlet of his reclining-couch.

It was a terrible finale; it was hung with not a tatter of dignity; it was crude, bloody, and pitiless. The terrified boy rushed to the couch to find that the knife had been removed from its sheath. Treacherous fingers had been at work even under the Imperial mattress! Holding Stephanus's blade somehow from his throat, Domitian howled for help, but these howls served only to hasten his end. For the wily steward had contemplated just such an emergency, and his fellow-conspirators were at hand. They were two young subalterns of the household guard—inflamed perhaps more by the Empress's arms than by the public weal—who had secured the approaches to the room. Maximus, a freedman, and a gladiator from the Imperial School were with them. Hearing the tumult, they dashed forward, and each, in turn, drove his sword into the body of the dying Emperor.

Thus Flavius Clemens, Domitilla, and many another were avenged, and Rome breathed more easily than it had done for some years.

The bias of early writing and tradition is towards the view that Domitian was a wholesale persecutor of Christianity. His name is bracketed with Nero's. But there is little evidence to support this charge. That he made savage and indiscriminate attacks, not only on Christians, but on pagans also, is obvious, and there was nothing in his conduct to stay excesses by provincial governors; yet one looks in vain for sign of a widespread and deliberate campaign aimed at destroying the new faith. His noxious personality, the exalted station of so many of his victims, and the fear he seems to have created on all hands may have contributed to the belief that he was a second Nero.

It is widely held that John was banished to Patmos during the reign of Domitian, a view which stems from a statement by Irenaeus that the book of Revelation belongs to that time; but, as already explained, a different interpretation is preferred in this narrative. No doubt Domitian was credited with homeless offences that needed to be laid at somebody's door, for he fully warranted detestation. It is little wonder that his most timely death should have brought the tolerant Nerva into power on a tide of reaction.

How warm a springtime the kind, sagacious influence of an elderly man can sometimes bestow on a winter-nipped generation! Nerva was between sixty-five and seventy years old when the Senate elected him to the purple, but he was no sooner established on the Capitol than bland sunshine seemed to drive away the chill from the ways of Roman life. Jurisprudence was Nerva's specialty, but all his instincts were humane and enlightened. He strengthened the authority and privileges of the Senate and unshackled the doors of those who had been unjustly imprisoned by his predecessor. Tears flowed from many a poor wretch whose eyes had not hoped to see the hills of Rome again or the open sky's delight.

The Lady Domitilla was freed from Pandateria, to be welcomed back by the pastoral arms of Clement. If the churches had had bells in those days they would have rung a jubilant peal.

17

The Unknown John

BUT some years earlier an old man more important than
any Roman Emperor had died at Ephesus. Amid all the
fanciful hero-worship of the early fanatics there is no real
assertion that John, the Beloved Disciple, met a martyr's death.
True, one later writer says so, but the claim can be forgotten
and his zeal forgiven. John seems to have died in his bed. The
orthodox view, based on the statement of Irenaeus, is that he
died in Trajan's reign, a near-centenarian. Insistence on extreme
longevity for various first-century characters appears in so many
primitive records that it must be regarded as stemming from a
desire to prolong association with the person of Jesus. In the
case of John there is evidence (summarized in Chapter 14) that
he was confused with his younger companion, John the Elder,
or Presbyter. If there is no written warrant for placing his death
in the time of Domitian there are reasonable grounds for believing this to have been the case. In A.D. 85—to suggest an
arbitrary date—those later personalities with whom he is
declared to have had contact could have been old enough
to have known, and subsequently remembered, him. If we are
to accept the view that he was by some years the junior of Jesus
—young, ingenuous, impulsive, and therefore sufficiently attractive to have won his Master's particular affection—he might
have been perhaps eighty years old in A.D. 85.

A pallet in a modest room close to the place of worship at
Ephesus probably saw the passing of John. If he had lain ill
for a time the leaders of the different Asian churches would
have come to take their leave of him. Was his old friend
Andrew, the other fisherman disciple from Bethsaida, still alive
to be with him at the end? These two had shared many wonder-

ful things in common. They had been followers of John the
Baptist before they were called by Jesus on that memorable day
beside the lake over half a century ago. Or was John the Elder
the only one long known to him who knelt beside his bed? John
the Elder would be grey-haired now: he too as a youth had
known the Christ; he had a disciple's rank. Philip the Evangelist
lived at Hierapolis, not many miles from Ephesus. Did he
come to receive the old man's blessing, or had he himself died
earlier?

One thing seems certain—that a boy of sixteen, very likely a
kind of acolyte either at Ephesus or Smyrna, would hear the
news of John's passing with intense grief. His name was Polycarp, and he had sat at the old Apostle's feet more than once,
listening to his stories of Jesus and his interpretation of the
teaching. Polycarp had like enough been with him when he
rushed from the baths because Cerinthus the heretic was inside.
At Antioch the news would come as a mystic challenge to the
heart of a fervent priest named Ignatius, who had not long been
converted to the faith and may well have received ordination at
the hands of John or Andrew, or John the Elder or Philip. In
the very earliest tradition Ignatius is spoken of as an "apostolic
man," meaning that he received his authority from one or other
of the Apostles surviving in his day.

What would not the world give to have but a little of the
knowledge which John carried in his memory to the grave?
Into his protection Jesus had confided his mother, Mary. Where
had she gone, where had she breathed her last? Had she too
spent her elderly life in John's care at Ephesus? Answers to
these riddles may yet be yielded up, for archaeology and chance
in our own century have provided more information than men
ever dreamed of concerning ancient history and religious
origins. For example, it was long held that, because of its
sophistication, the Gospel of St John must have been composed
at a very late date compared with the other three Gospels, but
papyrus fragments discovered in Egypt and in the John Rylands
Library at Manchester in the 1930's make it clear that the work
was in codex form around A.D. 150, and point to its having been
written before the end of the first century. At that time John the

Elder was alive, and these discoveries lend credence to the view that he was the actual writer.

Unknown but for the reference by Papias (quoted in Chapter 14), yet emerging more substantially in the light of scholarship and research, John the Elder must be considered one of the supreme disciples; for if he wrote the Gospel of St John he wrote what is by many considered the most important document in the New Testament. Here the person of Jesus Christ and the profound mystery of divine revelation are presented as in no other writing. The loftiest Christian judgment on it is summarized by Bishop Lightfoot:

> I believe from my heart that the truth which this Gospel more especially enshrines—the truth that Jesus Christ is the very word incarnate, the manifestation of the father to mankind, is the one lesson which, duly apprehended, will do more than all our feeble efforts to purify and elevate human life here by imparting to it hope and light and strength; the one study which alone can fitly prepare us for a joyful immortality hereafter.

What reconstruction of John the Elder can be made by a detective eye? On the assumption that he was the author of the Gospel of St John and the three Epistles of John, what kind of a man glimmers in the far shadows of time? By nature he was warm, tender, and earnest, yet he was not afraid to exercise the firmness to which his authority entitled him. In the third Epistle, addressed from "The Elder unto the well-beloved Gaius," he wrote: "Diotrephes, who loveth to have the pre-eminence among them, receiveth us not. Wherefore, if I come, I will remember his deeds which he doeth, prating against us with malicious words." Obviously, Diotrephes was going to get a dressing-down when the Elder arrived. The Elder had a more profound knowledge of Hebrew scholarship than the other Gospel-writers, and shows signs of being influenced by Hellenic Judaism. He wrote more discursively, from a subtler mind.

In the Gospel his aim is not only apparent on every page, but is deliberately set forth: "And many other signs [miracles] did Jesus in the presence of his disciples, which are not written in this book: but these are written that ye might believe that Jesus is the Christ, the son of God, and that, believing, ye might have life through his name." The central theme is love, and Christ as the personification and essence of love stemming from the Father. "O righteous Father," it records Jesus as saying in his farewell prayer, "the world hath not known thee, but I have known thee, and these have known that thou hast sent me. And I have declared unto them thy name, and will declare it; that the love wherewith thou hast loved me may be in them, and I in them."

The author everywhere selects, emphasizes, and concentrates in telling his story. He endeavours to provide a living picture of Jesus and to reflect the inner meaning of his teaching. It is as if he knew that the earlier writers—Mark, Matthew, Luke, and others now lost—had told the simple facts faithfully, but had failed to infuse their narratives with the divine mystery. To this shortcoming—aided by his own recollections and the more intimate remembrances of John the Apostle whom he had known so well and so long—he addressed himself. And he had the education and the religious understanding to complete the task effectively.

Purposive, learned, and affectionate—these were attributes of the man known as John the Elder. But there are two other clues. Polycrates, who was Bishop of Ephesus about a hundred years later, in his unreliable reference to John the Apostle, says that, "being a priest he wore the sacerdotal plate." If Polycrates was confusing the two Johns and putting on paper a tradition concerning not the Apostle but John the Elder, it might well be that the Elder belonged to a priestly family. That could account for his erudition, and it could also account for a notable feature of the Gospel of St John.

In this Gospel far more detail is given of those events that took place in Judaea and Jerusalem than in the other Gospels; the earlier, Galilean, part of the story takes a secondary place. Is it not conceivable that John the Elder, when little more than a boy, belonging to one of the rich sacerdotal houses in Jerusalem, joined the Nazarenes late in Christ's ministry, during the final drama at Jerusalem? His eager young eyes and ears would register just those little incidents taking place around him which he later incorporated in his report.

The writings of the Elder are linked by one significant common element. Like his friend and teacher, the Beloved Disciple, he was a resolute foe of the earliest heresy with which the infant Church had to contend. This heresy, one of the first advocates of which was Cerinthus, became known as Docetism. It held that the body of Jesus was not real; it was only an appearance, an illusion, without flesh and blood. As Jerome wrote long afterwards: "While the Apostles were still surviving, while Christ's blood was still fresh in Judaea, the Lord's body was asserted to be but a fantasy." How pugnaciously the Elder John resisted this theory and was continually aware of its propagation may be read in his words. At the beginning of the Gospel of St John is the famous phrase, "And the Word was made flesh and dwelt among us, and we beheld his glory. . . ." In the first Epistle of John is a similar declaration: "That which was from the beginning, which we have heard, which we have seen with our eyes, which we have looked upon and our hands have handled, of the Word of life. . . ." And again: "Every spirit that confesseth Jesus Christ has come in the flesh is of God; and every spirit that confesseth not that Jesus Christ is come in the flesh is not of God." The second Epistle has this: "For many deceivers are entered into the world who confess not that Jesus Christ is come in the flesh. This is a deceiver and an Antichrist."

Docetism became a formidable movement, and the orthodox seem to have called on all who had knowledge of the person of Jesus to help them to defeat it. It *was* defeated, but only after a protracted struggle which engaged the grave attention of the Church towards the end of the first century and during the first half of the second. Docetism, serpentine in its wriggles, took many forms and acquiesced in many modifications before it was finally destroyed.

It cannot be far wrong to place the first publication of John the Elder's writings between the years A.D. 90 and A.D. 95, and his death, "in the time of Trajan," around A.D. 99.

At the turn of the century Christianity, whose founder had been crucified only seventy years earlier, was known throughout the greater part of the Empire. Asia remained its most fertile ground, and Rome, though staking high claims from the Apostolic grandeur in which it had been born, was secondary to the more ancient foundations in cities like Antioch and Ephesus. But Christian associations had developed in Europe probably as far west as Spain and as far north as middle Gaul: they were established in the Eastern provinces, such as Galatia, Pontus, and Bithynia—populous regions round the Sea of Marmora and the Black Sea, including the glittering metropolis of Byzantium. The Mediterranean islands were virile centres of the faith. Titus, "mine own son after the faith," as Paul had called him, is said to have been the first bishop in Crete. Alexandria had a considerable Christian body, and churches had been organized in other parts of Northern Africa.

Just how these scattered and varied groups were administered it is not easy to judge. Even the term 'bishop' is confused with the terms 'presbyter' and 'elder,' and it is significant that when Clement wrote his epistle to Corinth it did not go from him as an individual bishop, but as from the whole Church in Rome. This suggests that, although they must have been, by character and galvanism, the leaders or shepherds of their flocks, bishops were not yet conceded the personal authority with which they were later invested. Formal worship appears to have been simple, set round a meal which, as a remembrance of the Last Supper, was an elementary Eucharist; and it is difficult to assess how far these services and gatherings had to be in secret. Christianity was an unrecognized sect; under Roman law its meetings came under the heading of unlawful association; and it has been pointed out by many writers that the silence of history in regard to the Christians generally at this period cannot be taken to mean that they were not hunted down and persecuted.

The truth is probably that conditions differed according to the characteristics of individual governors and magistrates. There was no telegraph, no radio, to transmit daily guidance from the Capitol. Nor is it easy to discover at what moment the Christians were recognized as being distinct—and profoundly different—from the Jews, whose religion was permitted. If any procurator chose to be ruthless against them the law was on his side. If he preferred to turn a blind eye on their peculiar, though kindly, ways the law took a holiday. On the whole, as amid the menacing temper Domitian had exhibited, it would seem that the Christians must have led a shadowed, discreet life, ever conscious that danger might flash suddenly in blade and thong; and many must have perished in local oppressions about which no record has come down to us. At the same time, Roman magistrates were accustomed to be tolerant. From the dignity of assured and world-wide power they could afford to allow the 'odd man out' his quaint pastimes or pursuits. This is what most of them probably did. Some outstanding personalities of the early Church can have survived only because they were regarded with that veneration which good and selfless people inspire in all societies where prejudice or malevolence do not prevail.

So through Nerva's brief but tranquil reign Clement at Rome, Evodius at Antioch, Aristion at Smyrna, among other bishops, ministered to their flocks; the converted priest Ignatius grew in fervour and eminence; the youth Polycarp reached a dedicated manhood. In Rome the mob shouted itself hoarse at the bloody displays in the grand new Colosseum. The Senate, more favoured than it had been for years, blessed the benevolence of the Emperor, and everybody was happy but the Praetorian Guard, who came to dislike the idea of serving a rather doddery sovereign. White locks and dim eyes do not appeal to restless, well-fed young warriors, however much they are agreed to belong to a decent old chap. But Nerva was not so purblind as they imagined. He knew his short suit and appointed the stern, brilliant soldier Trajan as his colleague and destined successor. That kept the legions quiet and pleased all Rome.

In a distant province the picture was different. To the civil administrators and soldiers in Judaea these affairs at Rome had an interest which was lost on the Jewish inhabitants, whose national life had been disrupted by the loss of Jerusalem and the destruction of the Temple. What was it to them that yet another military boss, buckled and clattering, had been man-oeuvred into position to put himself in a purple cloak when Nerva died? Roman arms had done their worst in Palestine. Over ruined Jerusalem the standards of the Tenth Legion still mocked them, and they were forbidden even so much as to approach the rubble that was once the City of David.

But the stamina and resourcefulness of the Jew were not extinguished, and his energy flowed along those courses that were still left open to him. Furthermore, he took a bitter satisfaction in the knowledge that Jerusalem itself had not fallen into the hands of Rome. It was not a city, but the grave of a city, over which the eagles glinted; the Tenth Legion sat fruitlessly on a stony mound, like a growling dog guarding a whitened bone. Let it growl!

Yet habitation of a sort must have been available in the environs of Jerusalem, if not within the broken city walls themselves; for little by little the Hebrew Christians from Pella and parts of Peraea drifted back. While the rest of the Roman world may have been at a loss to differentiate between Christian and Jew, the authorities in Judaea had a clearer perception. They may have observed the contempt with which orthodox Jews treated their Christian fellow-countrymen; at all events, they seem to have allowed Christians into the remnants of Jerusalem while keeping the Jews rigorously away at the point of the sword. This only increased the hatred felt by the dispossessed for these followers of the Galilean "Messiah"—these quisling friends of the oppressor—and the Romans were probably quick to realize that, by showing tolerance to the Christians, they were thrusting a new goad into the hide of the detested Jew.

Exactly when Simeon, the Bishop of Jerusalem, returned to the city is a matter of speculation, but that he did return somewhere about the turn of the century seems beyond doubt. Thirty years had gone by since the capitulation to Titus; another generation of young soldiers constituted the Tenth Legion; some reconstruction must have taken place among the wreckage. Simeon had been the leader of the Nazarene Christians for nearly forty years; he was now an old man. He and his friends came back to meet not merely the religious resentment but the thermal loathing of Jewry in general; and it cannot be denied that they must have accepted some sort of protection from the local Roman authorities. No doubt Simeon

was consumed with a desire before his own life ended to reassert
the cross where the crucified Jesus had suffered. That, of course,
would have to be done in the privacy of the congregation, and
not openly in such a way as to antagonize Rome; but at least
it could be done now without fear of those proud prelates who
had conspired Jesus's death. Like the Temple, the Sanhedrin
had been broken to pieces. With its disappearance the Sadducees
also disappeared, together with their privileged families who
had exercised power in Jerusalem for so long. The priesthood
too was a dying caste. Since the Temple and its altar no longer
existed it was not possible to offer burnt sacrifices to the Lord,
and the priests found themselves out of work.

This situation presented the Pharisees and Rabbis with a
matchless opportunity. They stepped into the place left empty
by the Sadducees and priests. They rallied the people to the
Law. It was the Law that mattered, not the Temple building.
In Rabbinic schools at places like Jamnia and Lydda flourished
Hebrew scholars of notable vintage, offering the disheartened
people a new kind of leadership. Among them none stood
higher than Rabbi Eliezer ben Hyrcanus, who was frequently
consulted by King Agrippa on matters of the Law. He was a
beloved old man concerning whom many references appear in
the Talmud, and at about this period when the Christians were
beginning to filter back towards Jerusalem a sensation was
caused by the news that Rabbi Eliezer had been accused
of displaying heretical conduct favourable towards Christian
teaching. He was brought before a tribunal of Rabbinic
elders.

"Does an old man like you concern himself with such silly
matters?" asked the president. The question suggests that the
proceedings were not taken too seriously; that Rabbi Eliezer's
offence was one of indiscretion rather than of purpose. So it
turned out to be. The charge was dismissed, but the venerable
Rabbi was deeply upset that he should ever have come under
suspicion; he could not, for the life of him, think how it had
occurred. When he got home his friends tried to console him.
Nothing availed until one of them made a remark that raised
an echo in the old man's memory. Rabbi Akiba suggested that

perhaps Rabbi Eliezer had at some time, in an unguarded moment, praised the saying of a Christian.

"Akiba, thou hast reminded me!" exclaimed Eliezer.

As his memory cleared he recalled how he had once been walking in the upper street of Sepphoris, in Galilee, when he met "a man of the disciples of Jesus the Nazarene," whose name was Jacob (or James) of Kephar Sechana. This Jacob had said to Eliezer, "It is written in your law *Thou shalt not bring the hire of a harlot into the house of the Lord thy God for any vow*. What then is to be done with it? A latrine for the high priest?" To this question Eliezer had made no reply, and Jacob had gone on to explain that Jesus of Nazareth, commenting on this same passage from Deuteronomy, had once said to him, "For of the hire of a harlot hath she gathered them and unto the hire of a harlot shall they return"—from the filth to the filth.

"The saying pleased me," said old man Eliezer to his friends, "and because of it I was arrested for heresy."

This sentence may be taken to imply that Eliezer had made reference to the saying of Jesus from time to time, and it had thus brought him under suspicion. The meeting at Sepphoris must have been some years before he was put on trial, otherwise he would not have forgotten it so completely until reminded by Akiba's remark. The conversational details thus recorded in the Talmud are a little obscure, but there can be no doubt that here, from a trustworthy source, is a fragment of a talk between Jesus and one of his followers of which no other account exists. The time factor does not present any real difficulty. Even if Rabbi Eliezer met Jacob of Kephar Sechana as late as the year A.D. 60 he himself would have been about forty, while a contemporary of Jesus need not have turned sixty.

Who was this Jacob, or James, of Kephar Sechana? The most eminent of modern Hebrew writers on the period, Joseph Klausner, has advanced the theory that he may have been James, the stepbrother of Jesus. Although James, at the time the conversation with Rabbi Eliezer must have taken place, was head of the Christians in Jerusalem, he was a native of Galilee—and that part of Galilee of which Sepphoris was the principal town. He would, no doubt, frequently return there. The village of Kephar Sechana is believed to be the modern Sukneh. These identifications are difficult, for Hebrew, Greek, and Arabic tongues have modified names over the centuries; but one alternative is at least worth postulating.

Five miles from Nazareth and an equal distance from Sepphoris stands one of the two villages considered to be the site of Cana of Galilee, where the water was turned into wine and where the nominal kinsfolk of Jesus appear to have had family associations. To-day it bears the name Kafr Kanna. The sound of that on the tongue is not very different from Kephar Sechana.

18

The Other Crucifixion

ANOTHER name rang with the metallic purpose of its owner. Trajan, who became Emperor in A.D. 98 on the death of the temperate Nerva, was a soldier from crown to toe; but he was less of a statesman than he imagined himself to be. He sought to secure Rome's power more firmly throughout the world and to draw the reins of government into his own hands. His fault was that he persisted in trying to bite off more than he could chew.

His clear-cut face was a determined one; resolution lay along the tight lips and in the upright furrows above his nose. But these last also indicated the frequency with which his brow was knit with the weight of those many problems he insisted on coming to him for solution. War was his *métier*; wherever his sword flashed he conquered; yet as his reign drew to a close the whole Empire was racked with tumult and unrest. Had Trajan understood more fully the art of responsible delegation his name might have glittered less dramatically in Roman military annals, but the Empire might have been stabler. Yet in himself he was composed, confident, tireless.

A practical, brave, and not intolerant man, he probably cared less for the things of the spirit—good or bad, enlightened or merely superstitious—than any of his predecessors save Vespasian. Emotion was a feminine frailty to which he was a stranger; cruelty a morbid pastime of which he was not guilty. In the first years of the new century he led his legions to great victories against the Dacians, riveting the Roman plate on remoter Europe. Then he turned his attention to the East, to the immense wastes of Parthia and Mesopotamia, hammering down opposition by tough encounter and clever manoeuvre. Having over many years spattered his greaves with Danubian mud and Arabian sand, he glimpsed India and sighed because he was not then a young man able to begin the conquest of further continents. All his Oriental triumphs were short-lived, insecure, a seed-sowing of revenge. Nevertheless, he was not neglectful of home affairs; he improved social conditions, kept faith with the Senate, and adorned Rome with a magnificent new Forum.

Time, which adjusts values and corrects enthusiasms, merely records these things. Trajan's arch and column symbolize his military feats; but they are only the tombstones of dead deeds, and he must have been, if not altogether unaware, at least unappreciative of those events that occurred during his reign which had a fertilizing power for future generations. A briefly dictated note to guide a distant governor—one of thousands he dispatched—a warrant, filed perhaps by some junior official in the State archives, a routine list of judgments from the proconsul of Syria—these formally embodied those things under Trajan which have occupied men's attention ever since, while battles along the Euphrates are forgotten and Dacia and Parthia have vanished.

The Emperor was away on the European front, eating his pork and cheese with the troops, when yet another cross was hauled creakingly into position on one of those tragic slopes near Jerusalem. Fastened to its beams was the old bishop, Simeon, son of Cleophas, cousin of Jesus.

Only a year or two had passed since his return from Pella, but the affronted Jews had found their opportunity to destroy him. The charges are known; the circumstances which enabled them to be pressed home can only be surmised. Jewish sectaries gave information to the occupying power that Simeon was of the line of David and might, therefore, lay claim to the throne of Israel, and, further, that he was a Christian. It is hard to believe the authorities in Jerusalem did not know perfectly well that Simeon was a Christian leader; perhaps in their Roman eyes the fact had been a recommendation because it angered the Jews. But, of course, if a charge was made in due form, and if confession was exacted, the law had to be applied and the penalty was inescapable.

L

There is just enough circumstantial evidence to presume a mean plot against Simeon which provoked the Romans to contempt. Hegesippus the sole authority for what is known, says that his accusers also suffered arrest for being themselves of the royal Jewish house "when search was made at that time for those of that family." In other words, despising the venomous motive of the Jewish complainants, the Romans ferreted out similar charges against some of them. One can almost hear the officer who first received the accusation saying to his subordinates, "Go and see what you can discover about these fellows who want to kill a harmless old man."

According to Hegesippus, the trial was held before Atticus, the proconsul, and this suggests it was taken out of the hands of the local Judaean magistrate. Simeon was tortured for several days before he was crucified, bearing himself with such fortitude that Atticus was moved to express his admiration. The torture might have been applied either to extract information about his fellow-worshippers or to force a repudiation of Christ. It did not succeed, and, like James the Just before him, Simeon, the cousin of Jesus, died near the place where his Lord and kinsman had died on the first Good Friday.

Simeon is declared to have been a hundred and twenty years old when he was crucified about A.D. 104 or 105. Of course, he may have been a venerable man, but this fantastic assertion must be put down to that fibbing which tried to establish contemporaries of Jesus. He need have been only in his early thirties when he was proclaimed Bishop of Jerusalem in A.D. 62, for thirty was recognized as an age when men were deemed worthy of episcopal leadership. Assuming that his father, Cleophas, was a man in his forties at the time of the Crucifixion, his son could well have been born a year or two before that event, and may have been a little child known to the Saviour—for all we know one of those who were blessed, as recorded in the Gospels. By this reckoning Simeon would be in his late seventies when he was martyred.

Another Hebrew named Justus was chosen by the Christians in Jerusalem to be their head. Great courage would be required to accept such a nomination in that faithful, now fugitive, community; for the execution of Simeon was a sinister portent, and not only in Judaea. Informing became a practice in many parts of Asia. The conclusion must be that the growth of Christianity had begun to worry administrators, and that they encouraged people to lay information.

As the churches spread and the years passed, so the personal picture changed. Clement of Rome had died in A.D. 101. Evaristus succeeded him, and he in turn was followed by Alexander in 109—the fifth bishop to occupy St Peter's chair. New men were devoting themselves to the study of the faith and its founder. Among these was Quadratus, who won shining eminence in Asia for his writings and interpretations. He affirmed the permanent nature of cures effected by Christ, declaring that he himself had known some of those who had been healed. Chronologically it is quite feasible, and it makes a unique point in the Christian argument.

But these men, and others equally devoted, who pressed onward with their liberating work—bishops, deacons, presbyters, and many women, like the daughters of Philip at Hierapolis— living under deepening threat, exercising the nerve-wracking wariness of the oppressed—all these made but the choired background to the next great acts. For two immortals were moving forward to complete, in tragic splendour, the drama of the Apostolic age. The fiery Ignatius was Bishop of Antioch; the beloved Polycarp was Bishop of Smyrna.

19

The Colosseum

HIGH above one of the gates of Antioch, beside the Imperial tokens, glowed a golden cherub. With other treasures it had been looted from the Temple at Jerusalem and presented to the city by Titus when he and Berenice celebrated the victory there. All who passed under it were thus reminded of the penalty in store for those who rebelled against Rome, while for marching soldiers it glittered by way of inspiration, large with promise of reward for duty gallantly done. Units of the army constantly passed to and fro beneath that gateway, for Antioch was the military headquarters of the East. Three regular legions had their depots and arsenals in the immense *campus martius* across the river Orontes, where trumpet-call and armourer's hammer sounded a familiar daily tattoo.

Perhaps half a million people lived in Antioch. The dust of many roads, the thunder of massive traffic, converged on it. Spectacular theatres, temples, and baths were clustered about its slopes; its famous colonnaded avenues were crowded with a volatile, Aramaic-speaking population amid which dashed the chariots and curricles of its Roman and Graeco-Roman aristocracy. There was much wealth here and plenty of that social gaiety inseparable from a great military centre. Officers by the hundred, many of equestrian rank, flocked into the city for amusement. Entertaining on a lavish scale must have been ceaseless in the villas and surrounding estates, while for the less scrupulous the beautiful gardens of Daphne offered erotic pastime and display three or four miles away beside the slow-flowing Orontes. At Daphne rose the temple and shrine of Apollo, set in fragrant groves and circled by murmuring streams.

Here on festal nights license did not pretend to stop at the obscene. Harlotry and its elaborations flourished around Antioch as in few other places of the Roman world, ebbing only when the legions were reduced by the demands of distant war.

A vivid, spendthrift capital, where fortunes were made and lost no doubt with equal rapidity; a gay, soldierly, vulgar but highly sophisticated resort, rowdy, laughing, and reckless, where love-making, wantonness, the clash of arms, and the brutalities of drunkenness swept the day into night. A hot, quake-ridden place where life was preferred in its more perilous aspects; where, from time to time, Emperors came in robed and generous triumph or, sword-on-thigh, called out the Eastern cohorts.

Febrile and acrid like the city whose name he bore was Ignatius, the Bishop of Antioch. Although his origin and the precise span of his episcopate are unknown, he is revealed with almost crystal clarity in his authentic writings. He commands the awe —and the reverence—due to a man genuinely consumed of Christ. He is forbidding, almost frightening, in his sacrificial devotion: the mind conceives him as an upright figure, hollow-cheeked and blazing-eyed, striding fearlessly to the doom assigned. Out of the crucible that was Antioch it seems fit that such a being should leap, carrying high the cross that had found refuge there in the earliest days, where the name 'Christian' was first adopted, where now the needs of the Church seemed to demand an attacking zeal.

Every clue suggests that Ignatius was converted in maturity. His words bear the seal of one whose life, transformed by some shattering experience, was thereafter passionately dedicated. In phrase and thought he emulates St Paul, as if he had trodden his own road to Damascus. He was a visionary; his fervent eyes saw what others could not see; he comprehended heavenly things, "the arrays of the angels and the musterings of the principalities." Like Paul, he knew what it was to be caught up into the pale of the divine. He refers to himself as "the last" and most unworthy of the Antiochene Christians, meaning that he had accepted the faith late in life; but his tortured professions of humility seem to meet a kind of arrogance in conviction. At one point he says, "At present it is far better for me to be timid and not to give heed to them that puff me up." A little later, "Pardon me, for I refrain lest you be choked by what you cannot receive."

Was Ignatius an evildoer, fleshly and corrupt, before he knelt to receive from an Apostle's hands the guerdon he so steadfastly maintained? It is probable; he shows a kinship with others whose ways were drastically changed, and the ferocity of his belief is typical of the reformed sinner. But in fact we know nothing about his early life. He was not a Roman citizen, for his subsequent treatment by Rome makes this clear. On the other side, his name is Italian. He could have sprung from a slave family. His eloquence must be rated high, and he was certainly not without education. It is a fair speculation that he was raised in comparative affluence amid the teeming, hybrid life of Antioch. His conversion may well have been recognized in the city as a victory over an individual of some consequence and, perhaps, some notoriety. Otherwise his speedy elevation to the bishopric—at only one remove from St Peter—is difficult to understand despite his virile personal qualities. One must assume that he had administrative ability; his constant love for the Church at Antioch is beyond question.

What brought him and his followers into open collision with the authorities is unknown; but need it be regarded as too baffling a mystery? It is impossible to credit Ignatius with temporizing discretion. Some flaming indictment of the amoral life around, even a bold condemnation of Roman officialdom, would not be beyond him. Such a man was bound to hit out sooner or later. Had he been a soldier he would have belonged to the *panzer* school: there was no Maginot Line in his philosophy. Moreover, he hungered for personal martyrdom so that he could be deemed worthy of his Saviour. To die gloriously he would live dangerously, and he carried the Antioch Church impetuously along with him. Debate continues about whether his behaviour stemmed altogether from purest devotion or whether vanity also had a strong grip on him. Would any man, in an age ill-equipped for publicity, pursue vanity to a shameful and terrible death?

In or about the year A.D. 108 action was taken against the

Christians in Antioch. It came significantly at the beginning of
a persecution which spread eastward to Pontus and Bithynia in
the years following; but in itself it seems to have been an
isolated event, in all likelihood provoked by the bishop himself
and his ardent presbyters. A number of church leaders appear
to have been arrested and condemned as well as their head, for
although Ignatius makes no mention of them, he rejoices to
learn a few months later that "the church which is in Antioch
in Syria is in peace," and the implication is that a persecution
had continued for a time and had then ended.

Legend contends that Ignatius appeared before the Emperor
Trajan in person at Antioch; this is demonstrably false. Trajan
was in Rome at the time. It was the pacific period between his
European and his Oriental campaigns. No; the Bishop of Antioch must have been brought in front of the Imperial legate
there—a viceroy enjoying one of the most exalted stations in
the Empire, having in his hand the balances of war and peace
in the East, and most certainly those of life and death for an
individual. Of the judicial proceedings nothing is known, but
the sentence is unchallengeable. Presumably Ignatius was
charged as a Christian; he must have refused to disavow his
unlawful faith, refused to scatter incense to the Roman gods,
and was sentenced to death. He was ordered to be taken to
Rome and, subject to the Emperor's will, to be devoured by
beasts in the Colosseum.

Nothing that had gone before exceeded the gigantic character
of the bloody scenes in the Colosseum at this time. Almost
daily large numbers of wild brutes were slaughtered, gladiatorial battles were staged, and human victims were burned alive
or tortured to provide "Roman holidays" for the excited mob.
From the farthest Imperial bounds, lions, panthers, and other
creatures were sent to Rome to meet the increasing demand.
Dio Cassius states that in the games of A.D. 106, organized to
celebrate the Dacian conquests by Trajan, 11,000 animals were
put to death. Colonial governors can have had few more
constant worries than those arising from the ceaseless forays to
capture beasts for the Colosseum; and the supply of human
victims became equally a matter of concern. At all costs the

mob must be propitiated, and its taste now was so contemptible that only an ever-more profligate blood-shedding could appease it. Every ingenious trick was perfected by which pain could be made manifest. Every possible device was used to cater for sadistic lust. A fanatical, pigheaded Christian was just another to toss into the glutted arena.

The day came when Ignatius, shackled to a soldier and in a military escort consisting of a maniple of ten men, was led out of Antioch on the long road to Rome. We have no means of judging his age other than by the strong presumption that he became a Christian in adult life and was admitted to the Church by some Apostolic person. On this basis he may reasonably be deemed in the region of sixty-five when he was arrested. Nothing in his own later writing, or in the fanciful legends about him, suggests he was aged or infirm. Mentally he was alert and potent, as his letters prove; he must have been physically robust to have stood the ordeal by road and sea that lay before him.

Tramping so many miles a day, perhaps in company with other prisoners, he seems to have been escorted along the northern road through the Cilician Gate, over the mountains to Laodicea, Hierapolis, Philadelphia, and Sardis to Smyrna, where a stay of a few days was made. The distance covered in this part of the journey was six hundred miles. It was made in the heat and dust of summer, when the sun beat down on the shelterless upland tracks. It must have been hard going, made harder by the soldiers' blackmail.

Custom allowed payment by prisoners to their escorts or jailers in return for little favours, and no doubt Ignatius had provided himself with bribe-money which the practised guards knew how to extort at frequent intervals. Later he wrote: "From Syria to Rome I am fighting with wild beasts by land and sea, by night and day, bound to ten 'leopards,' and they become worse for kind treatment. Now I am the more a disciple for their ill deeds, 'but not by this am I justified.' "

The word "leopards" here clearly means the ten soldiers. It is the first known usage of the word in Greek or Latin writing. Efforts to trace a Roman regiment or legion whose insignia was

the leopard have failed; it may be that at this time leopards
were considered to be among the fiercest beasts performing in
the arena, and Ignatius used the term to emphasize the particular harshness of which he complains. He would not be
entitled to any privileges, for in Roman eyes he was no more
than a routine prisoner. Inheriting as we do a long conception
of a bishop as a venerable figure in cope and mitre, it is not easy
to bear in mind that Ignatius was, to his captors, just another
crazy sectarian, wearing a common white *pallium* and a coarse
cloak, trudging along amid, perhaps, a few criminals, a cart or
two, and a small mule-train.

But the Christians in Asia took a different view. The grape-
vine had pulsed. News that the dynamic Bishop of Antioch was
on his way to die at Rome had flashed along the by-ways, and
when he arrived at Smyrna it was to be told that delegations
from the churches at Ephesus, Magnesia, and Tralles were coming to meet him there.

In some room at Smyrna, shuttered from the blazing mid-
summer sun, Ignatius clasped the hands of Polycarp, Bishop of
Smyrna. It would be an emotional moment for both men. They
had not met before; they were never to meet again. The ranks
of those who had known the Apostles were thinning; on these
two lay a heavy burden of responsibility to maintain the true
teaching and purge the churches of dross. Polycarp was now
about forty years old, carrying in his vigorous mind many a
precious recollection of John the Beloved Disciple and John the
Elder, and perhaps of Andrew and Philip. He was a man very
different from Ignatius. In Polycarp humility needed no conscious effort; it flowed through his nature. Tolerant, restrained,
more attached to the sweet savour of life and kindlier in judgment, he must have found Ignatius a disconcerting, if spell-
binding, visitor, freely granting him the seniority which his
approach demanded.

Some of the matters they discussed are not difficult to guess,
for they appear in Ignatius's later writings. War on the heresy
of Docetism must be relentless; both bishops were worried by
that doctrine. Episcopal authority must be more and more
recognized as the source of righteousness. As for the older man's

advice to the younger, it was given in a letter sent after he had left Smyrna:

> Vindicate your office with all diligence, both of the flesh and the spirit. . . . Be diligent with unceasing care. . . . If you have loved good disciples it is no credit to you; rather bring to subjection by your gentleness the more troublesome. Not all wounds are healed by the same plaster. Relieve convulsions by fomentations. . . . Be sober as God's athlete. . . . Stand firm as an anvil which is smitten. . . . Be more diligent than you are.

Although this letter expresses the writer's gratitude and loving devotion, and his glory on beholding Polycarp's "blameless face," it is easy to note the sting in some of these phrases, as if Ignatius, with his quick, remorseless eyes, had noted those little failings in Polycarp which make him the more human person.

They were joined by others of the church at Smyrna. These included a devout woman called Alce—"a name beloved to me," wrote Ignatius—Eutecnus, Daphnus, "the incomparable," and Attalus, "beloved." Presently the delegations from other Asian churches arrived. From Ephesus came its bishop Onesimus, a deacon named Burrhus, Crocus, Euplus, and Fronto. Burrhus later accompanied Ignatius on the next stage of his journey. His is a name that occurs in an early apocrypal book known as the *Acts of John*, where John is said to have ordained a deacon in Asia called Burrhus. Could they be the same? The church at Magnesia sent Damas the bishop, Bassus, Apollonarius, and Zotion. Polybius, the bishop of Tralles, also hastened to Smyrna.

Here was, in effect, a little convocation, and it must have held earnest debate—a debate invested with poignant solemnity by the reason that had led to its assembly. The soldier responsible for Ignatius, if not consistently chained to him, would have to be present—unless, as one suspects, he was bribed to drink his red wine in an adjacent room. The whole stay at Smyrna may, indeed, have been extended by the Christian leaders offering a rich reward to all the ten "leopards." It can be presumed they were neither worse nor better than Roman soldiery in general, and would not care a tinker's curse whether the cash came from Christians, Jews, receivers of stolen property, or procurers so

long as there was plenty of it. In Smyrna there would be probably less military oversight on such a band than in a more
important centre like Ephesus. The chance of a nice bit of
'lolly' would be worth taking. In any case, though the "leopards"
were, perhaps, too ignorant to realize it, they certainly allowed
their prisoner to fraternize with an illegal sect.

While in Smyrna Ignatius dictated four of the seven letters
which have been ratified by time and scholarship as authentic.
They were addressed to the churches in Ephesus, Magnesia,
Tralles, and Rome. In three cases they were not only parting
words of exhortation and advice, but of thanks for sending their
representatives to meet him. They contain repeated warning
against Docetism—the theory that Christ was not a real man
but a spirit, which had so gravely perturbed John and John
the Elder. In his letter to the Magnesians he writes:

> Now I say this, beloved, not because I know that there are any
> of you that are thus, but because I wish to warn you, though I
> am less than you, not to fall into the snare of vain doctrine, but
> to be convinced of the birth and passion and resurrection which
> took place at the time of the procuratorship of Pontius Pilate;
> for these things were truly and certainly done by Jesus Christ
> our hope, from which God grant that none of you be turned
> aside.

More emphatic on this theme are his words to the Trallians:

> Be deaf therefore when anyone speaks to you apart from Jesus
> Christ, who was of the family of David and of Mary, who was
> truly born, both ate and drank, and was truly persecuted under
> Pontius Pilate. . . . But if, as some affirm who are without
> God . . . his suffering was only a semblance, why am I a prisoner,
> and why do I even long to fight with the beasts? In that case I
> am dying in vain. Then indeed am I lying concerning the Lord.

The letter to the Romans is different. It casts an arresting
gleam not only on another matter that must have been discussed
by the gathering at Smyrna, but on Ignatius's character and on
the methods of communication available to the Christians. It is
an earnest, a desperate, plea to the Church at Rome not to
appeal for clemency for the writer. Obviously some of the
devoted company that had gathered to meet him at Smyrna had
begged him to allow them to write to Rome, calling on the
Christians there to do all in their power to save him from death.

There were influential persons among the faithful at Rome. Nerva, for example, had restored the Lady Domitilla to liberty; many people close to the Imperial family were among her friends. It is likely enough that letters had already gone to them, beseeching assistance for the Bishop of Antioch. But Ignatius would have none of this. In dictating his corrective admonition to Rome he revealed the depth of his unearthly passion. Surely this document must be reckoned among the greatest in the archives of mankind. It was flung down in haste, in magnificent temper.

> Ignatius, who is also called Theophorus, to her who has obtained mercy in the greatness of the Most High Father . . . to the Church beloved and enlightened . . . which has also the presidency in the land of the Romans . . . I am afraid of your love lest even that do me wrong. For it is easy for you to do what you will, but it is difficult for me to attain to God. . . . Neither shall I ever have such an opportunity of attaining to God, nor can you, if you be but silent, have any better deed ascribed to you. For if you are silent concerning me I am a word of God; but if you love my flesh I shall again be only a cry. Grant me nothing more than that I be poured out to God while an altar is still ready; that, forming yourselves into a chorus of love, you may sing to the Father in Christ Jesus that God has vouchsafed that the bishop of Syria shall be found at the setting of the sun, having fetched him from the sun's rising. It is good to set to the world towards God, that I may rise to him.

That kind of carping criticism which has sought to make Ignatius a little lower than the noblest is routed by the reckless language with which he proceeds:

> I am writing to all the churches, and I give injunctions to all men, that I am dying willingly for God's sake if you do not hinder it. I beseech you, do not "an unseasonable kindness" to me. Suffer me to be eaten by the beasts through whom I can attain to God. I am God's wheat, and I am ground by the teeth of wild beasts that I may be found pure bread of Christ. Rather entice the wild beasts that they may become my tomb and leave no trace of my body; that when I fall asleep I be not burdensome to any. Then shall I be truly a disciple of Jesus Christ when the world shall not even see my body. Beseech Christ on my behalf that I may be found a sacrifice through these instruments. I do not order you, as did Peter and Paul; they were Apostles, I am a convict; they were free, I am even now a slave. But if I suffer I shall be Jesus Christ's freedman and in him I shall rise free.

Now I am learning in my bonds to give up all desires. . . . Grant me this favour. I know what is expedient for me; now I am beginning to be a disciple. . . . Let there come on me fire and cross, and struggles with wild beasts, cutting and tearing asunder, rackings of bones, mangling of limbs, crushing of my whole body, cruel tortures of the devil, may I but attain to Jesus Christ! The ends of the earth and the kingdoms of this world shall profit me nothing. It is better for me to die in Christ Jesus than to be king over the ends of the earth. I seek him who died for our sake. . . . The pains of birth are upon me. Suffer me, my brethren; hinder me not from living, do not wish me to die. Do not give to the world one who desires to belong to God, nor deceive him with material things. . . . In the midst of life I write to you desiring death. My lust has been crucified and there is in me no fire of love for material things; but only water living and speaking in me, and saying to me from within "Come to the Father." . . . I write this to you on the 24th of August. Farewell unto the end, in the endurance of Jesus Christ.

Note how he put down the date. The letter was to go by the fastest possible route, at high speed along the Christian grapevine, so that it should reach Rome before he himself arrived and stop any disposition to false kindness. The date would be a check on the efficiency with which it was carried.

Within a few days of its dispatch Ignatius himself must have set out on the next stage of his journey, for the ten soldiers and their train could not tarry overlong. Parting blessings would be given and received, but sorrow and tears belonged only to those who remained behind at Smyrna. For Ignatius joy lay ahead. On through the scorching late-summer days he and his guards made their way to Troas, in the brown-baked land near the Dardanelles. Part of the way they may have gone by coasting vessel. At Troas good news was waiting. Philo, a deacon from Cilicia, and Rhaius Agathopus, from the Syrian church, had arrived to tell him that the persecution in Antioch was over and that his own church was living in peace again. Ignatius quickly dictated letters to Philadelphia and Smyrna, asking that each community should hasten to send deacons or ambassadors to encourage the weakened church at Antioch. In a last message to Polycarp he wrote: "You ought, O Polycarp, most blessed of God, to summon a godly council and elect some one who is very dear to you and is zealous, who can be called God's courier.

Appoint him to go to Syria to glorify your zealous love to the glory of God. . . . Farewell in the Lord."

This was a very hasty note, as the context well shows. He explains that the ship in which he and the soldiers were to travel to Neapolis had received sudden sailing orders, and he had not time to write to all the other churches about Antioch's need. He asked Polycarp to do it for him.

Thus, his mind filled with hopes for his beloved and famous church at Antioch, Ignatius left the Asian shore. One man would watch the vessel's sail dipping down below the verge, knowing how much of human stature and courage she was carrying. This was the deacon Burrhus from Smyrna, who now speeded back with Ignatius's letters and news of his departure. From Neapolis the "leopards" and their convoy marched to Philippi, where they were joined by other prisoners destined for the Roman amphitheatre. Then all is silent. The bishop's fevered voice is not heard again, nor, but for an inquiry from Polycarp of the Philippians, does factual history add anything more to this story. But it is the silence of accomplishment— accomplishment confirmed by all tradition.

As he had desired, so Ignatius was thrust out one day upon the saturated sand of the Colosseum arena, and there, under the fixed gaze of many thousands, he was put to death. After reading his letter to the Romans can anybody doubt but that it was with head high and hands outstretched that he faced the snarling animals, creeping ever closer? Maybe the eleventh leopard was among them, to receive a special greeting.

In the earliest times Ignatius's martyrdom was celebrated on October 17. It has been pointed out that, allowing for brief delays *en route*, the six or seven weeks between August 24, when he was at Smyrna, and the middle of October would just suffice for the journey to Rome, and that this date might be reliable. Trajan had been given the title Caesar and proclaimed Emperor in the month of October. Was it at some festival held in honour of that auspicious day that Ignatius died? If so, the Emperor may have been in the royal box at the Colosseum. He was not a vindictive man. But this was the Roman way of life, carried on bridges of death.

20

The Tortured Land

EVERY successful man depends on his portion of good luck. He draws on it a little whenever he makes a venture. But there are some who contrive to get a share even when playing for safety. Like the Vicar of Bray, they manage to hold their livings when more virile personalities are removed. They are not the makers of history, but they are its touchers-up. Of such was Pliny the Younger.

Discretion and adaptability were his watchwords. He always flowed on the day's tide, but never too obviously in midstream. He was not physically strong; his throat and chest gave him constant trouble, and he had to avoid violent exercise. Therefore he played those cards that nature had bestowed on him without leading the suit in which he was weak. No man can be blamed for that even if it takes the heroic out of his behaviour.

During Domitian's heyday Pliny held responsible office both in Rome and Syria. In Domitian's last years, when the shadows cast by public detestation lengthened ominously, he adroitly retired into private life, spending happy hours in the company of such distinguished men as Tacitus, Suetonius, and Martial. On Trajan's becoming Emperor Pliny emerged from his seclusion, and in A.D. 100 he delivered a eulogy due to the new *princeps*. It was marked by scathing denunciation of Domitian, his late employer, and fulsome and florid praise of Trajan, from whom he had hopes of employment. Could it sensibly have been otherwise? A few years later—in A.D. 111—Trajan showed his confidence in Pliny by sending him out as governor of one of the most restless regions in the Empire—Bithynia and Pontus. Here was advancement indeed, and the diligent proconsul was fully appreciative. He knew his master liked to exercise as much direct control as possible, and he began by referring all kinds of matters for his opinion or decision. No doubt he felt that a modest display of ready subordination would be profitable in the long run.

If he was one of the most forceful, Trajan was also, in some respects, one of the most long-suffering of Emperors. As Henderson says, "He pursued a lonely way through a troublesome world always with a somewhat enigmatic smile lurking about his lips." But Pliny's persistent correspondence about trivialities must sometimes have removed that smile. Nevertheless, only once is there evidence of mild exasperation, when, on being asked about repairing the baths at Claudiopolis, he replies, "You are on the spot and in the best position to decide." Otherwise, if succinct, he is always patient with "my dear Pliny."

Ever a disciplinarian, Trajan set prime store by the Augustan Law of Associations, framed to prevent the formation of societies or guilds that might become centres of disaffection. Pliny was anxious that he should do nothing to arouse his employer's mistrust in this direction. After a disastrous fire he asked if it would be in order to establish a properly equipped fire-brigade. The answer was a polite no: the risk of creating a corporate body was too great. Let property-owners acquire the necessary apparatus to protect their own premises, and if a serious conflagration broke out it was the governor's duty to muster all citizens. Even in the case of a Bithynian city, which enjoyed the privilege of a special charter, Pliny felt it wise to consult the Emperor before giving permission for a subscription supper to be held.

Yet it is entirely due to this careful man's letter-writing that we have any knowledge about one of the most sombre events in ancient history. His large province was being bathed in the blood of Christians.

The persecution seems to have been in full spate when Pliny arrived; its continuance and the cause of it presented him with a serious problem. The faith had spread through Pontus and Bithynia to such a degree that pagan temples were deserted and the State religions largely unobserved. Christianity must have numbered its adherents, nominal and sincere, by thousands in the principal cities—a condition which lends significance to the belief that it had been established there by Apostolic power, and is to be seen in the light of the tradition that St Peter himself had travelled there. Peter's epistle had been addressed to the inhabitants of these regions, and even at the time it was composed, around A.D. 65, they were suffering.

Some yet unfathomed mystery broods upon it all. If persecution had begun in Nero's time and had continued intermittently for more than half a century, fighting an obviously losing battle, the tenacity of the Church is evident. Massive authority at its founding and continuing inspiration in its leadership are suggested. Perhaps one or more of the twelve disciples whose names vanish from the record so quickly after the day of Pentecost lived and taught for many years in these Eastern provinces. Thomas, for example, is legendarily credited with having gone to the East—Thomas, who had doubted the Resurrection until he had felt Christ's wounds and had fallen at his feet crying, "My Lord and my God!" *There* was a man equipped to sow living seed!

Pliny had never faced a situation such as this. Local administrators were endeavouring to stamp out endemic Christianity by the process of bringing to trial all those who confessed the unlawful name; and so grave had its proportions become, they were rounding up suspects on generalized charges. The governor was not inhumane. He wondered if the desired end might be achieved by less rough-and-ready methods. He wanted clarification of the law. He was sincerely oppressed. If some of his other appeals for guidance from the Emperor seem to concern very petty affairs the letter he wrote about the Christians was fraught with importance.

In it he put three questions to Trajan. Was the age of a Christian to be taken into consideration, or were the very young to be treated as adults? Should a one-time Christian who recanted before the judge be pardoned? Did the name 'Christian' alone, apart from any other offence on its bearer's part, merit punishment? For the Emperor's comments he explained the system he had adopted. He had asked the prisoner whether he or she was a Christian, and if the answer was "Yes" he had

M

repeated the question again twice, with the warning that death was the penalty. If the prisoner continued to reply "Yes" to the charge he had been sentenced to death. Guilty persons who were Roman citizens had been remanded to Rome for judgment.

But, "because the investigation was going on," Pliny had found that accusations multiplied and that ever larger numbers were brought under suspicion. He referred to a list of alleged Christians that had been supplied by an anonymous informer. The persons named in it had been brought to trial, and he had felt justified in acquitting those who denied they had ever been Christians, who repeated a prayer to the Roman gods, offered wine and incense to Caesar's image, and cursed the name of Christ. Others agreed that they had once been Christians, but were no longer so; a few of them contended that they had abandoned the faith as long ago as twenty-five years. These all cursed Christ on being asked to do so.

More recent apostates, in defence of past misdeeds, said that all they had ever done was to assemble before dawn on certain days, praise Christ, pledge themselves to avoid adultery and crime, and reassemble later in the day to eat a meal together. (Here is another glimpse of the early Eucharistic rite.) But, asserted the prisoners, their meetings had ceased when Pliny published an Imperial decree forbidding secret societies.

Pliny went on to tell the Emperor of his personal efforts to find out more about the sect. He ordered two slave-girls "who called themselves deaconesses" to be brought before him. In his presence the girls were tortured, but even during their agony they had revealed nothing more than that they were addicted to a "depraved superstition." In other words, no dangerous political significance could be read into their practices or gatherings.

"I have therefore adjourned proceedings in order to consult you," went on the governor's letter. The whole matter, he urged, was an important one because of the great numbers of people concerned. They were of all ages, both sexes, and of every social condition. The Christian superstition had infected cities, villages, and the countryside; nevertheless, Pliny felt that, as a result of his method, it was reasonable to believe that it could be cured. He was able to report that the temples were no longer deserted, as they had been, and that Roman sacred festivals were being revived. A great mass of people, he felt sure, could be reclaimed from Christian perversion if they were given the chance to recant.

Trajan's reply was as follows:

> You have taken the right course, my dear Pliny, in investigating the cases of those charged before you as Christians. No universal fixed rule can be laid down. Search is not to be made for them. If they are accused and found guilty they are to be punished; but with this proviso, that if a man denies he is a Christian and gives proof of it by adoring our gods he shall, by this repentance, receive pardon, no matter how suspect he may have been. Anonymous accusations must not be heeded. They are a bad precedent, inconsistent with our times.

By this famous rescript Trajan confirmed the existing law, but insisted that it should be temperately and judicially applied. Evidence must be clear and full opportunity must be offered for recantation. It is astonishing that some eminent historians should have interpreted it as the initiation of oppressive measures and held that Trajan thereby devised a means of persecution. It was not so. He defined for Pliny's guidance the rule that had prevailed all along: Christianity was an unlawful, because it was an unauthorized, religious association. There were, in fact, other Oriental and Egyptian cults equally illegal, but they were not developing into Empire-wide movements and action was rarely, if ever, taken against them. There was nothing of the persecutor about Trajan; his rescript is a model magisterial pronouncement. Yet in his reign this tragic Bithynian blood-letting was executed. How long it continued, how many died, cannot be told; but that it was severe is evident. It must have shaken the Eastern Church profoundly.

Persecution seems to have broken out in other places as fear, and accompanying hatred of Christianity, developed. In the following years Asia suffered from serious earthquakes, and these were sometimes blamed on local Christians and their evil superstitions. Anything which suggested that the gods were angry brought sword and club upon them.

In A.D. 113 the Emperor, though now sixty years old, launched his ambitious campaign against Parthia. He made his head-quarters at Antioch, whence, a few years earlier, Ignatius had been taken to martyrdom. In the following winter he stayed there.

At daybreak on December 13 a terrible convulsion shook Antioch; the earth heaved and sank. Houses, temples, and public buildings crashed down amid the shrieks of the population. A third of the city was laid in dust and ruin, and thousands of people died, including one of the Roman consuls, Pedo Vergilianus. The Emperor himself escaped only because his guards led him to comparative safety in the open. It is quite possible that another persecution fell on the gallant Church of Antioch as a result of this visitation; for, as Tertullian wrote later in the century, "If the Tiber rises, if the Nile fails to rise, if there is no rain, if there is an earthquake, a famine, or a pestilence, the cry is immediately 'The Christians to the lions!'"

But nature's fury did not deter the practical soldier. Trajan launched his legions against Parthia's hosts and drove them like chaff before him to the shores of the Persian Gulf. Then the tide began to ebb with the ebbing of his own energies. Though he gripped Mesopotamia, his grip was not strong enough to endure. As the cohorts turned westward again the conquered peoples reasserted themselves in harrying units. Trajan put a nominee on the throne at Ctesiphon, but he did not rule for long.

During the winter of A.D. 116–117 Trajan once more lived at Antioch. The city had resumed its customary gaiety, and he and his officers had been received as brilliant conquerors, to be fêted and to be offered all its spicy relaxations after their months of battle. But as the late winter rains swept down sinister news came from all quarters. Everywhere the Jews of the dispersion were avenging themselves on the Roman world. They helped to attack Imperial garrisons left behind in Mesopotamia; they burst out in a fanatical massacre of Gentiles in Egypt, Cyprus, and Cyrene. Palestine itself and Libya were also infected. The pent-up wrath of the Jews vented itself in appalling barbarities. Dio Cassius declares that in Cyrene they ate the flesh of their victims, besmearing themselves with their blood. Twenty-four thousand non-Jewish inhabitants of Cyprus are said to have been slaughtered. Salamis, the capital, was plundered. Trajan commanded instant and stern repressive measures, sending the cruel Lusius Quietus to Mesopotamia with orders to destroy the Jews there, and Marcius Turbo, under similar instructions, to Cyrene. Hardly had these steps been taken before couriers from Britain came with tidings that the northern tribes there had risen in bloody revolt. It seemed that all Trajan's efforts to discipline the Empire had been but provocative of perilous reaction.

Worried and dejected, he knew that he must return to Rome to direct affairs from the centre. In the summer of A.D. 117 he set out from Antioch, but anxiety had done its deadly work. At the little town of Selinus, on the Cicilian coast, he had a stroke, and he died there on August 8. Before his collapse he may have learned about a disaster that haunted Rome's soldiery for years and remains to this day a mystery locked in the lonely Yorkshire fells. From York the famous Ninth Legion (Hispana) marched out in full battle order to subdue the Brigantes, who had taken up arms against the Empire. Some six or seven thousand strong, the veteran cohorts with their eagles took the road into the borderlands of Roman power. Not a man was seen again; not a whisper came back to tell how they had died. The Ninth Legion was buried for ever in silence and was struck from the roll of Imperial formations.

This frightening catastrophe focused the gaze of Trajan's successor on that distant frontier where fear stalked amid forest and ling.

21

The Traveller

SO, in the year A.D. 121, Hadrian, the new Emperor— Imperator Caesar Trajanus Hadrianus Augustus—looked over the ramparts of York, musing on the mysterious fate which had befallen the proud Ninth Legion. By now the Brigantes had been crushed: all was quiet under the eyes of watchful garrisons. But the Emperor knew that this quietude was illusory. In contrast to his predecessor, he had no conquering ambition—only a livelier sense for security. He was in his forties, with a powerful physique, and if he was to enjoy a peaceful reign in order to engage those interests which he preferred to war he knew that the Empire's defences must be consolidated.

Out of the Rhineland Hadrian ordered the Sixth Legion to march to York, to replace the vanished Ninth, and he commanded that a wall should be built from the Tyne to the Solway —a wall with strong points from which trouble on either side could be tackled, marking the Imperial limit and dominating the entire region. It was, in fact, a seventy-mile-long Roman fortress that could be neither surrounded nor totally carried by storm; an object on which hostile tribes could vent their spite and their energies to their hearts' content. Thus occupied, they would have no time or strength to indulge in dangerous penetration southward.

Hadrian's Wall was a bait for barbarians; to-day it is a curiosity for the tourist—though still empurpled when August brings the heather to bloom. Appropriate month, August! Perhaps in that season the spirit of the restless, quizzical Emperor sits on its stones, mildly approving the visitor who taps and prods them with his walking-stick. For Hadrian was an inquisitive, ever-travelling, inexhaustibly *interested* man. If he came to no particular conclusions about life it was not for lack of gathering knowledge—especially for seeing places and people with his own eyes. He prodded everywhere and asked questions in almost every part of the civilized world.

Although the cousins were closely attached, Hadrian was a very different man from Trajan. Trajan's energies were concentrated in a few channels; Hadrian's were dispersed in many. He loved literature and was highly skilled in Greek; he was an able musician; his interest in jurisprudence was deep; he was generous as a builder both in Rome and Athens. He kept a most watchful eye on the efficiency of the army, even though war did not appeal to him. ("When you charge you must ride knee to knee; I do not favour open order," he wrote to a cavalry regiment.) He was a broad-minded and humane man, capable of fun, wit, and common sense. Much more erudite than Vespasian, and having a far wider range of interests, coupled with a fastidious revulsion from excess, he nevertheless showed a similar vein of shrewd humour.

It was his habit to go to the ordinary public baths. One day he saw an old soldier there, rubbing himself against the wall. "Why do you use the wall as a scraper?" he asked. The veteran replied that he could not afford a slave to do it for him. So Hadrian gave him a slave. But when next he visited the same baths he found a lot of old men, who had been told of his generosity, rubbing themselves sadly against the wall. The Emperor had them assembled before him and explained that if they rubbed one another they could overcome their difficulty.

He derived much amusement from talking to people in the street; and though abstemious himself he enjoyed entertaining his friends at rich banquets. Urbane, sceptical, friendly, Hadrian knew the art of living, but above all things he liked to travel and acquaint himself with the fascinating world in which the gods had so admirably placed him.

In early manhood he had been married, largely by the well-intentioned manoeuvres of Plotina, Trajan's wife, to a girl twelve years his junior who was of so different a calibre that it is not

surprising they failed to get on harmoniously. She was Vibia
Sabina, whose statue confirms what the Court gossips wrote
about her. It is that of a pert, pretty, wilful, childish woman,
quick to pout and constant in demand for attention. In amusement, no doubt, they could combine, but Sabina was not
equipped to understand her husband's inquiring mind, and she
was often left behind, to complain justly of loneliness, when he
went a-wandering. There is a hint that even when at home they
neglected each other's company, for in a delightful letter to the
widowed Plotina, whom he regarded as mother in more than
the adoptive sense, Hadrian reveals that Sabina was not with
him on his birthday :

"You know, mother, that to-day is my birthday. We must
have dinner together on my birthday. Please get ready and
come with my sister as early as you can. Sabina is away in the
country. but she has sent me her own birthday present. Come
then quickly, as quickly as ever you can, that we may spend
the happy day together."

After leaving Britain in A.D. 121 the Emperor pursued a
leisurely way through France, Spain, and Portugal. Two years
later he visited Ephesus, going on to Pontus and Bithynia, where
the much-persecuted Christians seem now to have been living in
peace. He would be the last man unnecessarily to disturb them.
Then he returned to Asia, calling at one city after another,
studying the architecture, garrisons, local customs, and religious
rites. Late in A.D. 125 he arrived at Athens, touring the towns of
Greece. including Corinth. He made a journey to consult the
oracle at Delphi; but Eleusis seems to have held the most
fascination for him.

He showed on this and on a subsequent stay in Attica that
his eclectic mind had more than a passing regard for religious
matters. He stayed at Eleusis long enough to become an initiate
in the mysteries of its famous temple worship—esoteric and
ritual mysteries about which even now little can be comprehended. He also showed favour towards the Dionysiac celebrations at Athens. It is clear that Hadrian never committed
himself fully to any belief in the supernatural, but it is equally
clear that he found the subject continually worthy of his closest

attention; and he did not fail to return to Eleusis, after an appropriate interval, for the second stage of initiation.

This was in spring A.D. 129. All unconscious and careless that it was exactly one hundred years since the crucifixion of one Jesus whom the Christians worshipped, a sophisticated Roman Emperor, decked in symbolic saffron, moved through the columned Telesterion at Eleusis, a full member, or *epoptes*, of its inner circle. But did even the Christians themselves—for example, in that church at Corinth just across the water—realize that it was the centenary? On their part could they have cared less what nonsense the Emperor indulged in so long as he left them alone?

From Greece Hadrian continued his journeyings in the East, staying at Ephesus and visiting Cappadocia before returning for a spell to Antioch. In the following spring he went southward, Egypt being his objective. On the way he decided to have a look at the celebrated ruins of Jerusalem, that erstwhile capital that had once played quite a part in history.

So the day came when, accompanied no doubt by the governor of Judaea and the commander of the Tenth Legion, he examined what remained of the Holy City. In its hovels and battered ways he saw emblems of an epoch-making Roman triumph over barbarian superstition. A few impoverished Jews hung around the perimeter, clinging to the site of their primitive worship. Maybe he turned a not disinterested, if amused, eye on those Hebrews who believed that Christ had been their promised Messiah and derived compensation for their present miseries in the hope of joy when they were dead.

But in all this decay, simmering with yesterday's perversions as a corpse is prey to festering corruption, he saw a source of infection. Titus had punished Jerusalem terribly; the eagle had torn it to shreds. For half a century it had lain part buried in the putrefaction of death. It was time finally to bury these bones and raise above them a true Roman memorial. Before leaving for Egypt the Emperor gave orders that Jerusalem should be rebuilt in dignity and splendour, not any more as Jerusalem, the home of Jehovah, the rallying-point for Judaism, but as a Roman city. It should bear the name Aelia Capitolina to emphasize Imperial decree and a lineage from the Tiber, and where the Hebrew Temple had stood there should be raised a shrine of Jupiter.

Here was one of two extraordinarily ill-advised decisions made by Hadrian. The other was an order forbidding circumcision. This was not really directed against the Jews, but was intended to stamp out everywhere a practice thought capable of monstrous misuse, like castration, which had already been made illegal. But, of course, to the Jews it was a dire blow and insult, blunderingly timed. Coming just when the first stones were being shaped to house the worship of Jupiter on the spot where only the God of Israel had been adored hitherto, it fanned embers of hate that were presently to burst into consuming fire.

Hadrian moved blandly on to Egypt. Perhaps he was more intrigued by some aspects of life in the Attic society he had recently enjoyed; for it was on his cruise up the Nile that the affair of Antinous reached its climax. The Empress and her retinue joined Hadrian for the Egyptian tour, but whether her physical charms prevailed against the appeal of this Greek page is questionable. Antinous, a youth of excessive classical beauty, was accidentally drowned in the river. Perhaps, under the adulation he received, he thought he was Narcissus and fell in; we do not know. But Hadrian's grief was passionate and therefore significant. He turned it into a kind of grotesque sublimation which may well have drawn laughter from the practical and provocative Vibia Sabina. She was, after all, entitled to score a point.

The Emperor wept like a woman. He commanded that Antinous should be consecrated a god. Lickspittle soothsayers told him that a new star had appeared in the heavens and that it was the bright soul of Antinous. On the Nile's bank Hadrian founded a city called after him. His beauty was carved in hundreds of statues and shrines, and the poets had a busy time gilding it up in long-winded odes. The saddened Emperor returned to Rome, where in due course his grief subsided.

But hearts suffering a deeper woe and minds preparing a bitterer retort to fate now unleashed their passion. As Schürer says, "So long as Jerusalem lay in ruins the Jews could cherish the hope of its restoration. The founding of a heathen city, the erection of a heathen temple on the holy place, put an end to these hopes in terrible manner." In A.D. 132 the Jewish people rose in revolt which soon presented a situation as serious as that with which Vespasian and Titus had had to deal. It was different in character, and if, geographically, less widespread, was even more envenomed and elusive. It was a guerrilla war—possibly the most bloody of its kind ever waged. Though little detail has been preserved, the known facts are sufficient to establish its prolonged and sanguinary nature, and the deep anxiety it caused the Emperor and his advisers. For three years, amid constant fighting and frequent carnage, Judaea was really in the hands of the rebel leader, who seems to have been proclaimed by the Rabbis as the warrior Messiah, the new David, the liberator of Israel.

He must have been a towering personality, this rebel chief or prince, as he was styled: only a man of quite exceptional abilities and dominating presence could have led his people so skilfully or held out so long. His name is variously preserved as Simon ben Kosebah, Barcosiba, or Bar Cochbar. Where he came from, how he sprang forward at this critical moment, cannot be said, but he was high in rabbinical esteem. That he was ruthless and of iron will is apparent.

At the outset of the campaign he seems to have seized the site of Jerusalem—a startling feat when it is remembered that the Tenth Legion was in defensive position there. While he can hardly have maintained any permanent headquarters, for his whole campaign was organized in forays from the hills and assemblies in the lonely valleys, there must have been behind him some kind of executive group, for a pattern of government is glimpsed. Coins were minted, bearing the inscription "Simon, Prince of Israel," which suggest that he exercised considerable authority in an administrative sense for at least two of the three years. Certainly Rome cannot have held the power then.

Rome, indeed, was bewildered and temporarily beaten. Tineius Rufus, the governor of Judaea, soon found himself at his wits' end. The troops immediately available were quite inadequate, and a desperate call for help went galloping along the road to Antioch. Caius Marcellus, the legate, marched down from Syria in haste, with two, or possibly three, legions. Other formations were engaged as the struggle developed, and there is evidence that altogether soldiers from six legions took part, while units of the fleet are said to have been called out, possibly for landing operations against rebels on the coast.

Dio Cassius states that the Jews avoided meeting the Romans in pitched battle; they fortified all possible sites, using underground passages and caves as places of retreat, and swept down on the enemy from these positions whenever they saw a chance of punishing him. It was the kind of warfare the professional soldier detests—a murderous, quick-spearing, back-stabbing business of assault and retirement. The Roman generals were at a loss how to cope with it.

Worried by heavy casualties and the indecisiveness of the campaign, the Emperor himself left Rome and went to Antioch. Historians disagree about whether he actually participated in the fighting, but he seems certainly to have investigated the position at close quarters, and he made the decision that ensured victory.

Hadrian knew there was one Roman general long experienced in this kind of guerrilla struggle. The savage tribes in Britain used the very tactics that the Jews had adopted, and Julius Severus, the commander-in-chief there, knew all their tricks and how to smoke them out. Severus, probably at that time in the middle of a punitive expedition in Northumberland or Durham, must have been astonished to get the Imperial summons. He hastened to Judaea, and Hadrian gave him the supreme command. Within a matter of months the position was transformed, and Ben Kosebah and his bands found themselves in trouble. Gradually the Romans cleared pockets of resistance, and the rebels were hemmed in amid the caves and defiles south and south-eastward of Jerusalem.

In the year 1952, during searches instituted after the discovery of the first scrolls, there was found in one of these caves, near Muraba'at, east of Bethlehem, a letter on papyrus actually written by Ben Kosebah to one of his subordinates. John

Allegro, in his admirable book *The Dead Sea Scrolls*, offers this translation of the letter:

"Simon ben Kosebah to Joshua ben Galgola and the men of thy company; greetings. I call heaven to bear witness against me: *if* any one of the Galileans whom you have protected (or, delivered) cause trou(ble), I shall put fetters on your feet as I did to Ben Aphlul.—Simon ben Kosebah (. . .)"

Allegro points out that the letter is capable of a different meaning, and that Milik prefers the middle passage to read: ". . . *if* any of the Galileans who are with you are wronged I shall put fetters, etc."

Allegro considers that "the Galileans" were probably refugees; but is it not possible that they were Hebrew Christians? Might not the term "Galilean," which seems rather pointless in the text unless as one of reproach or sectarianism, have continued to be used when referring to followers of the Nazarene? There is reasonable evidence that the Jewish nationalists under Ben Kosebah vented their wrath on Christians, as Eusebius and Justin Martyr bear testimony, and it stands to reason that, apart from the gulf between them on doctrinal grounds, adherents of one Messiah could hardly be expected to tolerate the claims of another.

Even allowing for Dio Cassius's exaggeration—he declares that all Judaea was a desert after the war and that 500,000 Jews died—the land must have been cruelly impoverished; and as usual the Romans were merciless in the punishment they meted out. The building of Aelia Capitolina went on apace. Christian and Jew alike were affronted by the conquerors. On the Temple site the temple of Jupiter was built, containing a massive statue of Hadrian. Over the traditional tomb of Christ—and tradition at so early a date must have been very accurate—they raised a sanctuary for Astarte. A pig was carved upon the city's southern gate, and no Jew was allowed to enter on pain of death.

But before this Hadrian had returned to Rome, having satisfied himself that all was well in the capable hands of Severus. His journey back presents us with the possibility of a unique meeting between the purple and the Cross.

22

The Royal Court

AS Hadrian is known to have been back in Rome in May
A.D. 134, his journey from Palestine may be placed in
the earlier months of that year. Now fifty-eight years
old, he had seen more of the world, its peoples' virtues, frailties,
and foibles, than perhaps any other man alive. He had made
mistakes and learned to acknowledge them to himself. The
latest events emphasized how pertinacious men could be in
defence of their faith and race. The well-springs of human
motive must have puzzled and impressed him, as they do all
experienced and detached minds. A former governor of Judaea
had once asked, "What is truth?" What indeed? One knew what
expedience was and how, on occasion, it had to be sworded and
enforced; but about truth one could only speculate and be
tolerant as far as the needs of the State permitted. Well, such
as it was he had tasted life deeply. Now his body was not so
young as it had been. Walking twenty miles a day with the
soldiers no longer appealed to him. Now he would write and
read and talk and muse on many things at home in Italy. Above
all, he would be temperate in his judgments.

A Syrian inscription, "*pro salute Hadriani*," records that his
personal bodyguard spent a winter at Antioch. Did they observe
him in this kind of a mood as he started the homeward journey?
Did others whose prospects might benefit from Imperial goodwill seek his mellowing interest before he left the East at what
looked like, and indeed proved to be, the end of his last visit?
Was this the moment chosen by Christianity to put its case
to the Emperor?

Some years earlier Hadrian had written to Minicius Fund-
anus, governor of Asia, in reply to a request for guidance from

his predecessor who had been anxious about his duty in respect of Christians. This rescript is lighted with an even broader spirit than that of Trajan. If individuals came forward with precise allegations against specified persons it was in order, and a proper trial must be held. But Hadrian insisted that generalized complaints or entreaties were to be given short shrift: he stressed forcibly—"in the name of Heaven"—that false accusers should receive condign punishment for their wickedness.

The Emperor's credit as one holding a bridle on indiscriminate persecution was acknowledged; it moved some eminent Christians to believe that it might be possible to interest him in their enlightened religion. The first of many subsequent "Apologies," or reasoned arguments, on behalf of Christianity were addressed to him. One was presented by Quadratus, the Asian writer, and another by Aristides, an Athenian philospher who had been converted.

In what year or years did the climate become sufficiently moderate for these men to approach the Imperial majesty on such a forbidden subject? Quadratus is said to have handed over his Apology in Greece, but this statement seems to have arisen from confusing him with another Quadratus who became Bishop of Athens. It is more likely that Hadrian received him somewhere in Asia. At any rate, these occasions demonstrate that, in spite of the death penalty hanging over every self-confessed Christian, circumstances arose in which they were permitted to expound their doctrine to the throne itself. Some special dispensation could have been granted.

It is against this setting, misty but momentous, that the enigma of Polycarp and Florinus must be examined.

Fifty years after the revolt of Ben Kosebah the most famous second-century writer of all, Irenaeus, then Bishop of Lyons, wrote to reprimand an old friend named Florinus for holding heretical views. His letter contains this passage (the translation is Lightfoot's):

> . . . these opinions the elders before us, who also were disciples of the Apostles, did not hand down to thee. For I saw thee, when I was still a boy in Lower Asia, in company with Polycarp while

thou wast faring prosperously in the royal court and endeavour-ing to stand well with him. For I distinctly remember the incidents of that time better than the events of recent occur-rence: for the lessons received from childhood, growing with the growth of the soul, become identified with it; so that I can tell the very place in which the blessed Polycarp used to sit when he discoursed, and his goings out and his comings in, and his manner of life, and his personal appearance, and the discourses which he held before the people, and how he would describe his intercourse with John and with the rest of those who had seen the Lord, and how he would relate their words. And whatsoever things he had heard from them about the Lord and about his miracles and about his teaching, Polycarp, as having received them from eyewitnesses of the life of the Word, would relate altogether in accordance with the Scriptures. To these things I used to listen at the time with attention by God's mercy which was bestowed upon me, noting them down not on paper but in my heart; and continually, by the grace of God, I ruminate upon them faithfully. And I can testify in the sight of God that if that blessed and Apostolic elder had heard anything of this kind he would have cried out and stopped his ears, and would have said after his wont, "O good God, for what times hast thou kept me that I should endure these things!" . . .

This is, of course, one of the most important passages that have survived from the ancient writers. It paints a memorable picture of Polycarp, vigorous, diligent, persuasive, forthright; it confirms his acquaintance with John and, from that un-tainted source, establishes the accuracy of the Gospels. But so far as historical reconstruction is concerned, it is the first sen-tences that hold attention. When was this occasion in "Lower Asia"? What "royal court" passed that way, and in whose reign?

Irenaeus, the letter-writer, is known to have lived into the time when Victor was Bishop of Rome—about A.D. 190. Jerome says he was a prominent personality during the reign of the Emperor Commodus (A.D. 180–192). The date of his death is unknown, and these are our last reliable notices of him. His activity at a considerably earlier date is unquestionable. He had long been a presbyter when he was appointed Bishop of Lyons in A.D. 177; and it is a fair assumption that he died at an advanced age towards the very close of the century. In the letter to Florinus he says plainly that he was a boy when that particular meeting with Polycarp took place; it had obviously been a long, long time ago. If he was sixteen or seventeen then, and if he died between A.D. 195 and 200 when nearing eighty, his birth must be placed in the region of A.D. 115 to 120. He could well have been such a boy as he describes himself in the year A.D. 134, when Hadrian returned with his personal body-guard and his "royal court" from Judaea to Rome, taking the road through Syria and Lower Asia.

Florinus, a fashionable young courtier perhaps a year or two older than Irenaeus, was endeavouring to ingratiate himself with Polycarp. Why? For one in relatively close attendance on the Emperor it would surely be the height of folly to cultivate the principal leader of an illegal sect—unless, at that particular time and in that particular place, the Emperor was looking kindly on that particular leader. Can anything otherwise be deduced if Irenaeus's letter means what it says? It has been argued that the context does not necessarily imply the presence of the "royal court" at the town where Polycarp discoursed. But even if that be allowed the question has still to be answered, Why should an ambitious young man, "faring prosperously" in his heathen sovereign's eye, wish to curry favour with the most prominent Christian alive?

Was it not because Florinus was quick to sense those drifts of favour or disfavour that eddy round a dictator's throne; because he was eager to be where he would be approved for being, in the hope that another friendly smile might fall on him when next the Emperor passed? The use of the term "endeavouring to stand well" with Polycarp suggests that Irenaeus was being gently sarcastic about the not very exalted motive that first led Florinus to hear the word of truth.

It is difficult even to approximate to certainty, but this letter leaves a strong impression on the mind that the "royal court" had either received, or conferred some favour on, Polycarp. The speculation may be put forward that Hadrian had heard—indeed, he must have heard—about the renowned Bishop of Smyrna, for Polycarp's fame among the Christians was by now immense. Could it not be that, having pondered the Apologies

N

of Quadratus and Aristides, the Emperor summoned Polycarp in some Asian city which lay on his homeward route and invited him in person to amplify their arguments?

Moving through Judaea, the Decapolis, and Syria as he had done, Hadrian's interest in the Christian phenomenon cannot fail to have been stimulated, especially when he must have had many examples brought to his notice of the antagonism which the Jewish enemy showed to them. Under his authority the Christians of Jerusalem were treated with forbearance, and those that were Gentiles were allowed to settle in Aelia Capitolina, though Jews were rigorously excluded. This is a remarkable consideration in itself. It confirms earlier evidence that Rome had perceived the profound difference between Christian and Jew, and it suggests, further, that some thought had been given to the pursuance of the policy; for there was a world of difference between showing an expedient tolerance towards the sect in respect of ruined Jerusalem and granting them permission to dwell in the new Roman city—even if their shrines were later desecrated by Roman gods.

The paradox must be accepted that, while Christianity remained an unlawful association, its adherents were allowed personal liberties denied to the Jews, whose religion was not illegal.

One of those illogical situations had been created that are not uncommon under the stress of colonial administration. As the Emperor left on his journey back to Rome his mind must have revolved this among other aspects of affairs. To a man so apt to become temporarily engrossed in the speculative ideas of those around him the opportunity of gaining further knowledge may well have appealed. The fact that he had admitted the first Apologists is inescapable.

Smyrna, where Polycarp was bishop, lay on one of the overland routes to Rome—that tragic route taken by Ignatius and other victims destined for the Colosseum. It was in "Lower Asia" as defined by Irenaeus in his letter to Florinus. Here, if they did meet, was the obvious place; it was a recognized resting-point for those making the long journey. The local Roman military governor would have some modest *praetorium*, and within it we may conceive the Emperor and the Bishop to have come face to face. There is no record; it is a hazarded scene built from strands of circumstantial evidence. Polycarp was now aged sixty-five, a figure of experience and authority—to Christians throughout Asia the living embodiment of the faith that had been so intimately transmitted to him by the disciples.

It would seem that at the time he was delivering a course of lectures elsewhere in the city. This supposition emerges from Irenaeus's picture, which suggests a crowded hall, the discoursing bishop, his comings and goings as he moved from point to point among the audience. The young Florinus was present at some sessions, making his interest obvious, perhaps, by asking questions of the speaker. As a member of the Emperor's retinue, he would focus unusual attention when he spoke, and his eagerness to stand well with Polycarp impressed the lad Irenaeus looking on.

Hadrian's stay in Smyrna would not be protracted; he had to press on to the capital. In due course the Imperial cavalcade, shining in troop and chariot, rode out of the city. Polycarp could have been among those who watched it go. Hope would be in his heart that he had sown good seed to bear fruit in high places, and a benediction would certainly be given by that compassionate soul. More than quarter of a century earlier he had written to the Church at Philippi: "Pray for all the saints. Pray also for the Emperors, and for potentates and princes, and for those who persecute you and hate you, and for the enemies of the Cross, that your fruit may be manifest among all men, that you may be perfected in him."

But princes, like lesser men, come to dust and silence. Hadrian never travelled abroad again, and four years later, racked with merciless pain, he was carried to Baiae. There, on the golden shore where Caligula had dismissed Herod Antipas and the name of Jesus had first been spoken in Italy, he died. Polycarp remained.

23

The Lonely One

POLYCARP remained, and it was at once his glory and his cross that he had length of days. Seventeen years of life remained for him after Hadrian's death. During these years he not only grew in fame and veneration, but trod a road of increasing personal loneliness. All who grow old must experience the same profound sense of change. One by one cherished companions depart till the very idiom one has known fades echoing away, and every note and smile that has warmed life dies from sound and sight. But in Polycarp's case there was much more than this to bereave the mind and burden the heart. As his older contemporaries—many whose names are unknown to us —died he became in deepening solitude the repository of personal knowledge about Christian beginnings.

Men like Papias, Bishop of Hierapolis, though younger than Polycarp, had some once-removed links with the Twelve and had known secondary disciples such as the Elder John and Aristion; but they had not met John the Galilean; they had not, like Polycarp, heard voices that had been familiar in the ears of Jesus, nor looked on features he had loved. And Papias himself may well have died long before Polycarp's own life ended.

It is impossible to conceive any man in all history bearing a greater load of responsibility than that borne by Polycarp in the fourth and fifth decades of the second century. The Gospels had been published, the New Testament was complete, the record had been put down for ever. But how much of glowing personal detail was missing from these writings! "Let us ask the blessed Polycarp; he will know the answers," cried a fervent new generation. They must have swarmed about him from every eastern province, to touch his robe, to say they had seen him with their own eyes, to ply him with questions: "How did John the disciple speak? What more had he to tell about those magical days at Bethsaida and Capernaum? What did Jesus look like? Was he tall? Did he wear the *tallith* always? Was Judas Iscariot harsh of voice, as became the wretch? Who was present when Jesus went before Pontius Pilate? And Peter—tell us the way he taught. Did Christ break the bread this way or that? How did John interpret the parable of the king who went to a far country?" The contemporary mind has only to ask itself what burning demands it would make of one who had stood so close to the intimates of Jesus, were he by some miracle alive now.

The solitariness of kings has become a commonplace. In the ultimate they have nobody to share their function or resolve their decisions for them. On a remote peak, they are set apart. Yet what king was ever unique in this sense like Polycarp, Bishop of Smyrna, or was ever required to breathe the rarefied atmosphere of his towering isolation? For he was called on to influence not the immediate fate of nations, but, as he believed, the final destiny of mankind; and in many a circumstance his alone could be the judgment, his memory alone the fragile cord along which the truth must run. Though helped by early creeds, he must have prayed deeply—that he might firmly retain the Word, that he might not err in recollection through weariness of years, that he might fight the good fight according to his Master's will now that all the rest were gone and he had none from whom to seek advice.

Polycarp was not an Ignatius; he did not stalk like a flaming brand among men. The fight he fought was that of one faithful yet forgiving, humble yet constant. His letter to Philippi reveals his modest pastoral nature:

> These things, brethren, I write to you, not at my own instance but because you first invited me. For neither am I nor is any like me able to follow the wisdom of the blessed and glorious Paul, who when he was among you, in the presence of the men of that time, taught accurately and steadfastly the word of truth. . . . Knowing therefore that "we brought nothing into the world and can take nothing out of it," let us arm ourselves with the armour of righteousness and let us first of all teach ourselves to walk in the commandment of the Lord. Next, teach our wives to remain

in the faith given to them and in love and purity, tenderly loving
their husbands in all truth and loving all others equally in
chastity, and to educate their children in the fear of God. Let us
teach the widows to be discreet in the faith of the Lord, praying
ceaselessly for all men, being far from all slander, evil speaking,
false witness, love of money, and all evil, knowing that they are
the altar of God and that all offerings are tested and that nothing
escapes him of reasoning or thoughts, or of the secret things of
the heart. . . .

Let the presbyters also be compassionate, merciful to all, bringing back those that have wandered, caring for the weak, neglecting neither widow nor orphan nor poor . . . refraining from all
wrath, respect of persons, unjust judgment, being far from all
love of money, not quickly believing evil of any.

Yet there was about Polycarp nothing of that vapid acquiescence which is an attribute of stained-glass sanctity. In a few
words Irenaeus, his pupil, presents a memorable picture of him
hitting out when exasperated. "O good God!" it was "his wont"
to say on such occasions. One can see him thrusting a hand
through his white hair as he did so, in despair at the stupidity
or wickedness of men. Energy must have been his in abundance,
not only because he lived so long and was physically active to
the day of his death at the age of eighty-six, but because his
application seems to have been ceaseless. When he was well
turned eighty he made the gruelling journey to Rome in order
to wield a cudgel on a point in dispute with the Roman Church.
How many octogenarians are tough enough to make that
journey to-day, with all the amenities of modern travel?

Of what Polycarp wrote only the letter to Philippi remains.
The text of this, coupled with contemporary references to him,
strengthen the belief that he was not outstandingly erudite or
subtle. Goodness, rectitude, loving-kindness—these were his
qualities rather than the command of dialectic, yet as an utterly
trustworthy witness to the faith his continual attacks on prevailing heresies—which were largely variations of Docetism—
made him not only a formidable but a successful campaigner.
He recalled some notable heretics, followers of Marcion and
Valentinus, to the right belief. In his Philippian letter he wrote:
"Every one who shall not confess that Christ is come in the
flesh is antichrist, and whosoever shall not confess the testimony

of the Cross is of the devil." Here is an echo of one of his masters, the Elder John, who wrote in what we call his first Epistle: "Every spirit that confesseth not that Jesus Christ is come in the flesh is not of God; and this is that spirit of antichrist whereof ye have heard that it should come."

In its language Polycarp's letter to Philippi reveals also how familiar he was with the first Epistle of Peter, again emphasizing that document's importance to the Eastern Church, and certainly adding force to the claims for its authenticity. Would John the Beloved Disciple have encouraged his young followers like Polycarp to trust in a work bearing the name of Peter if it were not genuine? New Testament critics seem to have been oddly blind to this cogent argument. Polycarp, a simple man wedded entirely to all he had learnt in youth at the feet of disciples, a man who fought tenaciously against every deviation from the Gospel teaching, would look with a dubious eye on any writing that had not been approved by those who knew the truth. And he was steeped in Peter's epistle.

Polycarp's last journey to Rome must have been undertaken only a year or two before his death, for it was during the time when Anicetus was Bishop of Rome. He went to oppose the Roman observance of Easter.

Anicetus held the view that the anniversary of the Crucifixion should always be held on the Friday nearest to the 14th day of Nisan, the Jewish passover, and that the Resurrection should be celebrated always on the following Sunday—what we know as Easter Day. Polycarp protested that John and the other Apostles whom he had known had kept the 14th of Nisan in remembrance of the Crucifixion, independently of which ever day of the week it happened to fall on. Once again the faithful old man is seen battling for the tradition he had been taught from boyhood. Anicetus could not agree with him, and they parted without bitterness, but not before Anicetus had given a public demonstration of his humility towards Polycarp by allowing the Bishop of Smyrna to celebrate the Eucharist in Rome.

About this time younger leaders of the Church who were to achieve fame were present in Rome. They included Irenaeus and Justin, the great Samaritan apologist. It seems inevitable that Justin must have met Polycarp, either in Rome or in Asia, while from the pen of Irenaeus came constant testimony to the old bishop's steadfastness: "He ever taught those very things which he had learnt from the Apostles, which the Church hands down, and which alone are true." Irenaeus also described a dramatic meeting during that visit of Polycarp to Rome. Marcion, the most audacious heretic of the age, suddenly presented himself before Polycarp.

"Recognize us!" cried Marcion, arrogantly.

The old man looked him in the face.

"Aye." he replied, "I recognize thee—thou firstborn of Satan!"

Back over the long route Polycarp returned from Rome, possibly in the year A.D. 154; back to his flock at Smyrna, set in the midst of much pagan and Jewish activity. He was never to cross the sea again, for not long afterwards a letter broadcast among the churches brought tears and pride to the whole of Christendom. The letter has come down to us:

> The Church of God which sojourneth at Smyrna to the Church of God which sojourneth at Philomelium and to all the brotherhood of the holy and universal Church sojourning in every place; mercy and peace and love from God the Father and our Lord Jesus Christ be multiplied. We write unto you, brethren, an account of what befell those that suffered martyrdom, and especially the blessed Polycarp, who stayed the persecution, having as it were set his seal upon it. . . . For he lingered that he might be delivered up, even as the Lord did, to the end that we too might be imitators of him. . . .

24

The Pyre

IT was an early spring Saturday in A.D. 155. The sunshine
was already hot upon the Asian fields, and the hills above
Smyrna bore their yield of colour where the wild narcissus
and anemone graced the rocky slopes. Balsam and cedar, stirring to new life, freshened the woodland air. But all tracks leading into the city were throwing their dust into the rays of light,
for everybody from surrounding districts was going to the
festival—not least the Jews, who held a high sabbath. The narrow streets were packed with jostling, noisy crowds. Smyrna did
not boast avenues and buildings of renown like Antioch, though
its temples to the Augusti had some colonial fame, and sacred
games—the *Olympia Hadrianae*—had been graciously instituted there by the late Emperor on one of his visits.

To-day the main thoroughfare leading towards the great
stadium was kept clear of congestion for the legate of another
Emperor. Antoninus Pius now occupied the throne at Rome. He
had brought precious blessings to the Empire, and men were
destined to say that his reign marked one of the most beneficent
periods in the story of civilization. Peace and tolerance prevailed. The personal life of Antoninus itself was governed by
these conditions. He was a man of sterling character, upright,
merciful, studious. But what ruler of such an immense realm
could always be responsible for things done in his name, or even
hear their later echoes? Before night closed on this Saturday
events were to take place in Smyrna that would have grieved
and angered the Emperor had he known of them—this
Antoninus who encouraged Christian apologists, who had restored the rite of circumcision to the Jews, who sought to bestow
prosperity and tranquility on all his peoples.

His Imperial proconsul in Asia at this time, who administered the province from the *praetorium* at Ephesus, was Statius Quadratus. He had come to Smyrna to represent the Emperor at the games. On this Saturday morning early—for daily life in the East, whether for toil or for pleasure, began then, as it begins now, before the sun has climbed far—Statius Quadratus drove in state to the amphitheatre between applauding crowds and with an escort of soldiery. He entered the already crowded stadium in the company of the Asiarch, one Philip of the city of Tralles, who had prepared the entertainment and was responsible for its fitting production.

The Asiarchate was an office of the greatest dignity and consequence. In the Roman worship it embodied the high-priesthood of Asia. The Asiarch's duties were to promote veneration of the Emperors, to attend to the maintenance of their temples and shrines, and to lead the people in their adoration on festive occasions. In legal status he ranked near to the governor and had magisterial power. He was elected for a period of time, and was usually chosen from the richest in the land because he had to bear the expense involved in putting on games and other celebrations instituted by Imperial decree. Tralles was a wealthy city which had provided personal fortunes for many, and, as in the case of Philip, the Asiarch was frequently a citizen of Tralles, able to produce the means for lavish displays.

Naturally, at an event so notable as this the proconsul presided, and the Asiarch, sitting near him, took second place. Doubtless the games began with modest exhibitions of swordplay and manoeuvre while the people poured into position along the benches and banks, for the second-rate performer has always to pass the time till the house is full. As the day's warmth increased there would be fruit and wine for the distinguished visitors and their ladies, chatting away to fill in the hours before the highlights came on. Maybe the crowd grew restive, barracking and squabbling as it became uncomfortably packed. Later happenings showed that it was a ferocious crowd.

Thousands of Jews had come especially to whet their appetite on what had been promised. Amid them, and amid the indifferent holiday-making throngs of Levantine Greeks and Syrians, were others whose hearts beat fearfully and whose minds were laden with anxiety. For the Church of Christ was under persecution once again in these parts, and Christians had been brought for display at the games not only from Smyrna itself, but from places as far afield as Philadelphia. To these distressed onlookers every sound of trumpet fanfare and gong, every announcement from the Imperial dais, every impetuous shout from the mob, brought a breathless moment. What was to come? Lord! what was to come? Prayer, with which they dare not move their lips, pleaded for the prisoners. Their eyes searched the face of the proconsul seated up there, a dignified figure wrapped around in a toga freshly white from the fuller's yard. Would he be merciful?

A hush as the herald stepped forward into the arena to make a proclamation, then a great roar from the crowd, and the first Christian prisoners were brought face to face with the president, standing below his empurpled dais.

Statius Quadratus approached his duty with repugnance. In all that is told of him that day he stands out as a man who strove to save the captives from suffering and his own conscience from remorse. But humanity was not enough. He was in the clutch of circumstance. As an Imperial legate he had to uphold the law and sanction those punishments it provided. His behaviour was watched by tens of thousands whose demands, in so far as they were legitimate, must be met. On a high festival like this the people, enjoying their rights, expected also their sordid privileges.

As the prisoners stood before him Statius Quadratus went meticulously through the prescribed form. If they confessed that they were Christians he begged them to recant, pleading with them to see the folly of unnecessary sacrifice, warning them of the peril in which they found themselves, and trying, as it were by persuasive stages, to get them to utter the word or two that would have entitled him to set them free. It is easy to realize how restive the mob became while these interchanges went on at one distant point in the great stadium; easy to hear the cries and boos which filled the air when defiant gestures were made to which the uneasy proconsul seemed to reply with provoking mildness.

At last scourging was ordered for those who persisted in being stubborn—whether as a prelude to death or in a further effort to break down their resistance is not clear. From weighted thongs wielded by gladiatorial arms they underwent appalling laceration while the spectators roared and their quick blood-lust was kindled. In simple but ghastly terms the Smyrnaean Church afterwards described the scene: "Who could fail to admire their nobleness and loyalty to the Master, seeing that when they were so torn by lashes that the mechanism of their flesh was visible, even as far as the inward veins and arteries, they endured patiently?"

This was what the mob had come to see! This was not child's-play; this was getting down to real entertainment; nevertheless, there were many who wept for the sufferers and cried aloud in praise of their silent heroism as the whips rose and fell, perhaps rushing away from the amphitheatre when the inevitable cry arose, "Fetch the lions!" For everybody knew that the generous Philip, that excellent Asiarch, had hungry wild beasts in readiness down in the fetid pits.

"To the lions with the Christians!"

"Christians to the lions!"

Classic cry, known from coast to coast and province to province—it had to be obeyed, this voice of the people! And though Quadratus went on pleading with each prisoner in turn, the guilt that could not be gainsaid fell now to the dust in a smother of tawny flanks and bloody fangs, while the yells of the swaying multitude rose to the echoing hills. The sharpness of death, its sprawling finality, and the grotesque distortion of it vitalized their own delight in living.

Some of the twelve prisoners doomed to die faltered when they saw these things until they were inspired by Germanicus, one of their number. He was a man noble in bearing and comely to look on; he had some standing in the Church at Smyrna. Upon him the proconsul bent strenuous entreaty: perhaps Quadratus had sons of his own, straight-backed young men like this, in life's full springtime. But Germanicus refused to deny the Cross. Nothing could be done for him. A beast was turned loose which he fronted unflinchingly. Even then the proconsul tried a last throw.

"Have pity on your youth!" he cried aloud, distress making him unconscious of his dignity.

Germanicus answered by rushing upon the lion and dragging it towards him so that the end might be speeded.

It was then that a new, ominous murmur rumbled through the mob. "Polycarp—where is Polycarp, the ringleader?" Why should these hefty young fellows go to their deaths while the devilish old instigator of it all escaped? The idea passed from lip to glistening lip under cover of the general pandemonium, lighting up baleful eyes. Christian scouts, trembling, slipped away to warn and hide their devoted bishop. Would they dare to touch him? He had not even been charged. Surely it would be against the law? Quadratus could not permit it. But Polycarp must be got away, quickly! Through the streets they hastened while another incident in the arena fired the danger they had only glimpsed.

One or two captives had been burned alive to vary the sport provided by the Asiarch, and the stench of roasted flesh now drifted across the remnants of the dead on the reddened sand. All this horror was too much for a youth named Quintus. When his turn came he broke down before the lions could get him. A sharp command from the proconsul, and he was saved. Then, standing before Quadratus—who was doubtless glad in his heart to have preserved at least a solitary life—the lad cursed Christ, offered a whiff of incense to Caesar, and was set at liberty.

This must have brought a silence to the vast audience. As they craned their necks and watched him—tremulous, shamed, and distraught—being led away they were seized with a swiftly mounting passion to put the blame for such evil things in the right quarter, to bestow punishment where real guilt lay.

"Polycarp! Bring Polycarp, the atheist leader!"

In every quarter they lifted the cry. It bellowed from the corded throat of vengeance. They rose in their places gesticulating and demanding his blood. Only the death of Polycarp would satisfy them now.

This uproar alarmed the proconsul and the Asiarch: here was a development they had not anticipated. Such a menacing

tide could carry them into gross illegality. It was sternly forbidden by Imperial rescript to bring Christians to judgment on
a mere clamour. No man had dared to accuse the venerable
Polycarp. That was a very different thing from prosecuting a
few lowly Christians just to keep the movement in check.

Whether any effort was made to prevent what followed or
whether, indeed, the authorities openly acquiesced in it does not
appear. While tumult continued in the amphitheatre armed
horsemen set off to find and arrest Polycarp. The evidence suggests that from this time onward the proconsul and the Asiarch
took the line of least resistance, realizing that a perilous situation might arise if the crowd were deprived of its prey. Foremost
in zealous demand for Polycarp's death were the Jews, who had
reason to detest Christianity and were now recognized as its
most deadly smellers-out and hunters.

The old bishop was living at a farm on the outskirts of
Smyrna. When members of his flock rushed in from the
stadium to warn him about the rising temper there, and about
threats to his own person, he answered with resignation, "The
will of God be done." But the thought that he might come to
hurt—that the most beloved and venerated figure in Christendom should be at the mercy of those abusive fiends and their
obscene delights—was more than the faithful company around
him could contemplate. They compelled him to try to save
himself, and he was hurried to a small cottage some little distance away.

Hardly had this move been accomplished before his pursuers
galloped up to the farm. They found it deserted and began to
cast about for clues. In the adjacent fields they came across two
slave lads who had served Polycarp. The boys declared they did
not know where their master had gone till one of them, under
torture, revealed the truth.

A few minutes later the bishop's hiding-place was surrounded,
and, banging on the door, the men burst in. They seem to have
been joined by some officers of the city guard, perhaps to lend
formality to their proceedings, perhaps to see that no lynching
took place to the discredit of the Government. In the cottage
were Polycarp's friends, among them, no doubt, presbyters of

Smyrna. The intruders announced their mission and demanded the bishop's person; the whole scene would be one of rough entry and bitter manner, while in the yard outside horses stamped amid the rattle of accoutrements.

Now followed one of those moments when ignorance and brutality find themselves awed by the presence of a superior mind and a calmer will. Polycarp had been resting in an upper room. He came down. The rowdies fell silent when they looked on his gracious features at close quarters. He knew what they had come for, but the day was hot, and though it was now late afternoon there need be no reckless hurry. They had awakened him from sleep; he had not had time to pray for the world which he was about to leave so soon. Would they grant him an hour for prayer and in that time partake of his hospitality? Muttering, they agreed. He ordered a table to be spread with refreshment for them, and then stood up in the midst of his friends, remembering before God "all who at any time had come in his way, small and great, high and low, and all the universal Church."

Then he rejoined his captors, and they rode with him back to the city, more quietly than when they had come. In anguish and helplessness the Christians looked on.

Along the road the cavalcade was met by the chief of police, who bore the sinister name of Herod. He was accompanied by his father, Nicetes, apparently a substantial citizen. Nicetes is believed to have been a brother of that Alce, the devout Christian matron to whom Ignatius had paid tribute, and he seems to have been desperately anxious to prevent the threatened martyrdom. He and Herod took Polycarp into their own carriage for the rest of the journey to the stadium, and tried to prevail on him to save himself.

"Be sensible," they pleaded. "What harm can it do to say that Caesar is Lord and offer a bit of incense?"

For a space Polycarp was silent, meditating, while they drove on through the now levelling sunshine. Herod and Nicetes persisted in their entreaties, and at last he answered them: "I am not going to do what you counsel me." This stubbornness angered the two men. Had they not put themselves out to help

him? Well, let him go to the devil. From persuasion they turned
to threats, their temper rising until, when the carriage reached
the stadium, they were violent enough to shove him out so that
he bruised his shin.

News that the Christian leader had been brought in swept
through the shouting thousands like lightning and encouraged
them to a near-riotous frenzy. As the old man walked towards
the proconsul it was hardly possible to hear anything above the
din, but one voice was defined. It cried, "Be strong, Polycarp,
and play the man!" Afterwards the pious averred that it must
have been a voice from heaven because nobody had seen the
speaker, but it is more invigorating to believe that the words
came from some stout Christian with a muscular throat and a
valiant pair of lungs. Yet the Bishop of Smyrna had made his
resolution; his mind was composed and his strength of heart
was manifest to them all.

So he stood at last before Statius Quadratus, who must have
sat in ceremonial fashion, flanked by his glittering captains.
Under a belted surcoat the bishop would be wearing a simple
pallium. A spot or two of blood oozed from his barked shin; his
white hair drifted in the lazy wind. Perhaps he leaned a little
on a staff, for he was eighty-six years old. The low sun cast
quickly lengthening shadows.

"You are Polycarp?"

Identity was established, and the proconsul went on with the
formal examination, though he must have been worried by what
was pending, and, as the bishop did not fail to remind him, he
must have realized how hypocritical these proceedings were. For
when Quadratus called on him to show his loyalty and swear
by the genius of Caesar as Rome's divinity Polycarp replied, "If
you pretend that you are ignorant who I am, hear then plainly
—I am a Christian!" As if any one of the thousands rippling
the tiers of the auditorium did not know all about his renown
and the altar he served! The very idea was a preposterous sham,
worthy of a smile, if not a laugh. Had they not all recognized
him, howling like wolves, the moment they saw him in the
amphitheatre? He made a suggestion to the proconsul, whose
perplexity the old man seems to have appreciated.

"If you would learn the doctrine of Christianity assign a day and give me a hearing," he said.

This was a shrewd point; it must have renewed Quadratus's doubts concerning the propriety of what was going on. Would it not be wise to accept the offer? Due consideration might then be given, if necessary, to the formulation of a charge. The proconsul had only to say the word and, in effect, the Emperor would have spoken. But Statius Quadratus was not equal to this challenge. He feared the mob, packed so densely and so closely around him, more than he feared the possible reaction of Antoninus Pius in far-off Rome. Then suddenly a subtle way out presented itself. He indicated the shouting audience.

"Persuade the people of your doctrine, not me," he said, implying that they must be the judges.

The Bishop of Smyrna regarded him steadily.

"As for you," he replied, "I would have held you worthy of discourse; for we have been taught to render to princes and authorities appointed by God such honour as does us no harm. But as for these"—with a scornful gesture towards the *canaille* —"I do not hold them worthy that I should defend myself before them."

The proconsul fell to pleading. "Have respect to your age," he urged. "Repent. Say 'Away with the atheists.' "

Polycarp looked round him at the heathen ranks, raised his hand, and cried heartily, "Away with the atheists!"

Feeling that here was unexpected progress, Quadratus pressed him. "Swear the oath, and I will release you. Revile the Christ."

To this demand the old man returned a now immortal answer: "Fourscore and six years have I been his servant, and he has done me no wrong. How, then, can I blaspheme my King who saved me?"

In the end beaten, humbled, reluctant, the proconsul, after the appropriate words of warning, abandoned the case. It was over. The people were giving tongue in no uncertain way: they must be quieted. Three times a herald announced from the arena, amid a crescendo of abuse and satirical jeers, a proclamation that could hardly have been news to anybody: "Polycarp has confessed himself to be a Christian!"

o

"Turn the lions on him!" came promptly the vehement cry; but Philip the Asiarch, anxious, no doubt, to be quit of such guilt, declared that no lion could be loosed and that the games were over. Was the day not finished?

This ruling appears to have marked the end of control over the infuriated mob. Leaping the barriers, they took the law into their own hands. If there was to be no lion, who dare deny them fire? From the stadium workshops they snatched timber, and they brought faggots from the baths, vengeful Jews leading these raids. Polycarp was seized and hustled to a stake that had been erected while others hastened to and fro, building the pile.

He unfastened his outer cloak and girdle, and then, bending his worn frame, tried to take off his shoes. This action drew tears to the eyes of Christian onlookers, for it was many years since he had had to do such a thing for himself. It had been regarded as a privilege by the faithful to kneel before him and remove them, as it had been even to touch the hem of his garment. But now his hour had come.

Men approached with nails to pin his hands to the stake. He waved them off, saying, "Leave me as I am, for he that will enable me to endure the fire will help me to remain at the pile." So they fastened his wrists behind him and tied him to the beam with rope.

The day was far gone, and the Asian sundown was mounting its pomp of cloudless radiance over the darkening sea. A sudden hush dropped on the expectant thousands when men with lighted torches were seen running towards the staked figure. Polycarp lifted his face to the shining sky, and they saw his lips moving in prayer. Straining their ears, those who understood these things, and were near enough among many who had pressed forward into the arena, heard him pronounce the Gloria and the Amen. The pyre was lighted; the flames eddied and shot upward. Now the silence was broken deafeningly. The mob, dry-mouthed with lust, proclaimed their triumph. Their eyes devoured the sight of a frail old body shuddering through pain into ashes. It was nothing to them that the dissolving hands were the last that had clasped those which had touched the person of Jesus Christ. The physical link was broken in the fire, but the chain of sacrifice was forged anew that day at Smyrna, to endure and grow, century by century, into and beyond our own tortured times, till all shall be accomplished under the bright, the morning star.

25

Epilogue

THAT was the end of the beginning. "Be thou faithful unto death and I will give thee a crown of life" were words the visionary Christ of Revelation had addressed to the Church at Smyrna. Polycarp, Bishop of Smyrna, obeyed the command, and thus completed the laying of those foundations which it was the glory of the Apostolic Age to make firm for the generations to come. He might justly have echoed the prayer spoken by Jesus on the eve of his arrest: "I have finished the work which thou gavest me to do." Labouring in the still perceptible radiance of their tremendous leader, the disciples and their immediate followers accomplished a feat the results of which even they could hardly have thought possible.

It was done in a surprisingly short time. A homely example illustrates this. If we take the year 1958 as the equivalent of A.D. 155, when Polycarp was martyred, the Crucifixion would have been in 1832. Polycarp, aged eighty-six at his death, would have been born in 1872. John, the son of Zebedee, assuming that he was actually born in A.D. 5, which would make him seven or eight years younger than Jesus, and lived to around the age of eighty, would on this comparison have died in 1888, and John the Elder about 1899. In relation to our own time John the Apostle spanned years rather longer than, but similar in retrospect to, those lived, for example, by Robert Browning (1812–89). John the Elder would have died so recently as the very eve of the present century, which a multitude of people now living remember vividly.

The faith thus made fast to earth has become the dominant fact of history, something so immense and yet so familiar that its continuing marvel is apt to be overlooked. The course of the world for the past two thousand years can be seen to have meaning and coherence only if interpreted in terms of the Christian advance. Those vast international issues that afflict our generation arise from no other cause. So far as the mind can see, the future of Christianity must as certainly decide the fate of man —and perhaps that of the very globe he lives on—as its past has, more than any other influence, moulded his ethical conception, his social conscience, and his artistic expression.

Spiritual matters as such do not lie within the scope of history. Their objective manifestations do. In spite of many signs that there is in contemporary Christian communities what their leaders condemn as lack of faith, and a falling-away from former confidence, the longer view confirms that Christianity is the only religion that shows resurgent and conquering vitality. Many philosophies affirm principles, tenets, and forms of behaviour like those incidental to Christianity; but they have been unable to stand up to its compulsive appeal because they lack the central human-yet-superhuman force which Christians attribute to the person of the living Christ and which the uncommitted onlooker must concede to be unique.

In the story of Christianity that victory-out-of-defeat from which it sprang has been repeated again and again. There have been long periods of perilous setback. The toil, the agony, the endurance—often accompanied by bitterness and cruelty on the part of Christians themselves—have been on a prodigious scale. Recessions have been so severe and prolonged as to have seemed like final defeat—phenomena which those apprehensive about the present state of the faith should remember. Particularly grave was the long retreat between A.D. 500 and A.D. 1000. Of this half-millennium Mr K. S. Latourette (*A History of Christianity*; Eyre and Spottiswoode, 1954) has written that Christianity's

very existence was threatened. The decay of the Empire and the culture with which its phenomenal successes in its first five hundred years had almost identified it, seemed to presage its demise. Christianity's very victory appeared to have become its doom. The invasion of the Mediterranean world by non-Christians, notably by Islam-bearing Arabs, tore from Christianity approximately half the areas which had been gained in the preceding period. The morale of the Christian communities declined to their lowest ebb. . . . Never again since those long, agonizing centuries has the prospect for Christianity appeared to be so bleak.

The next four hundred years were of advance; then came another lesser setback before a further march of conquest, and so on. But the overall picture is of victory. In our day the establishment of Communism along vast reaches of territory offers a temporary barrier to the next offensive; yet there are now 820 million nominal followers of Christ—that is, one third of the world's total population. Every competitive movement in religion or philosophy has been left far behind. Its influence, pervasive, insistent, stems from a thousand effective centres; from such great sees as Rome and Canterbury, from the ancient patriarchates of the East, from priests of liberty, reciting daily the mighty articles of belief enshrined in the creeds; from pastors of the Free Churches of Europe and the United States, emphatic in preaching the Gospel.

But without those few workaday Jews who left their boats where the lake still frets on its pebbled shore how could this miracle have been done? Without those heroic hearts and strong hands that later built its deep walls when the architect was gone how could the Church have endured? Believers will call them instruments of Providence, but it is a terrible thing to be an instrument of Providence.

From Peter to Polycarp these men and women were of human bondage, subject to the various weaknesses that track us from the womb. Inasmuch as they were instruments lesser people, while revering them, must also pity them, for their lot was hard. Inasmuch as they were mortals caught up from their amiable lives to go a-soldiering in a tremendous campaign we must bow our heads before them. For no triumph has been like their triumph, nor did any other seed-sowing yield so great a harvest —pressed down and overflowing. They wrought in pain and passion long ago—so long ago that we are prone to forget they knew laughter as we know it, and kisses, and also the sweat of fear; that they were clothed in flesh no less sensitive than is our own to heat and frost and blade and whip. But they endured all things and never quit the field.

Sources and Acknowledgments

THE basic classical sources for this subject, apart from the New Testament itself, are, of course, the *Ecclesiastical History* of Eusebius, the *Annals* and *Histories* of Tacitus, the three books by Josephus, the *Twelve Caesars*, by Suetonius, and the writings of Dio Cassius, Pliny the Younger, and Philo of Alexandria.

Of standard modern works one stands out pre-eminently, and without its knowledge, wisdom, and exhaustive detail a writer attempting a narrative like this would be gravely handicapped. I refer to the massive *Apostolic Fathers*, by Dr J. B. Lightfoot, who adorned the See of Durham in the late nineteenth century. It rises above the achievements of others, and the reader will realize that I have made the fullest use of it. The writings of Harnack, Schürer, Milman, and Ramsay listed below are also indispensable, while that great Jewish scholar Joseph Klausner has in recent years contributed immensely to our general sense of the times and of the inner life and light of Judaism. The *Cambridge Ancient History* is naturally inevitable.

I have relied substantially on E. W. Henderson's splendid biographies of the Emperors listed below. English translations used in the text have been taken from several works, to whose authors and publishers I have expressed my indebtedness in the Preface.

ARNOLD, W. T.: *The Roman System of Provincial Administration to the Accession of Constantine the Great.*

CARCOPINO, J.: *Daily Life in Ancient Rome.*

CONYBEARE, W. J. and HOWSON, J. S.: *The Life and Epistles of St Paul.*

EDERSHEIM, A.: *Sketches of Jewish Social Life in the Days of Christ.*

FOAKES-JACKSON, F. J.: *History of the Christian Church from the Earliest Times.*

— *The Life of St Paul.*

FRIEDLÄNDER, L.: *Roman Life and Manners under the Early Empire.*

GOGUEL, M.: *The Birth of Christianity.*

GRÄTZ, H.: *History of the Jews.*

GWATKIN, H. M.: *Early Church History to* A.D. 313.

HARNACK, A.: *The Mission and Expansion of Christianity in the First Three Centuries.*

HENDERSON, B. W.: *The Life and Principate of the Emperor Nero.*
— *The Life and Principate of the Emperor Hadrian.*
— *Five Roman Emperors.*
KAUTSKY, K.: *Foundations of Christianity.*
KEIM, T.: *Rome and Christendom.*
KIDD, B. J.: *A History of the Church to* A.D. 461.
KLAUSNER, J.: *From Jesus to Paul.*
KNOX, W.: *St Paul.*
LATOURETTE, K. S.: *A History of Christianity.*
LIGHTFOOT, J. B.: *The Apostolic Fathers.*
— *Dissertations on the Apostolic Age.*
LIGHTLEY, J. W.: *Jewish Sects and Parties in the Time of Jesus.*
LOISY, A.: *The Birth of the Christian Religion.*
LOWE, J.: *St Peter.*
MERIVALE, C.: *The History of Rome under the Empire.*
MERRILL, S.: *Galilee in the Time of Christ.*
MILMAN, H. H.: *The History of Christianity from the Birth of Christ.*
MOMMSEN, T.: *The Provinces of the Roman Empire from Caesar to Diocletian.*
PARKER, H. M. D.: *The Roman Legions.*
RAMSAY, Sir W. M.: *The Church in the Roman Empire before* A.D. 170.
RENAN, E.: *Antichrist.*
— *The Apostles.*
SCHÜRER, E.: *A History of the Jewish People in the Time of Jesus Christ.*
SMITH, Sir G. A.: *The Historical Geography of the Holy Land.*
STREETER, B. H.: *The Primitive Church.*
WAND, J. W. C.: *A History of the Early Church to* A.D. 500.
WEISS, J.: *The History of Primitive Christianity.*
WEIZSÄCKER, C. VON: *The Apostolic Age of the Christian Church.*

Index